The History and Politics of Latin American Theology

Volume III
A Theology at the Periphery

Mario I. Aguilar

scm press

British Library Cataloguing in Publication data

A catalogue record for this book is available
from the British Library

978 0 334 04177 1

First published in 2008 by SCM Press
13–17 Long Lane,
London EC1A 9PN

www.scm-canterburypress.co.uk

SCM Press is a division of
SCM-Canterbury Press Ltd

Typeset by Regent Typesetting, London
Printed in the UK by CPI William Clowes
Beccles NR34 7TL

Contents

To José Aldunate sj, Dan Berrigan sj and
John Dear sj

Fortiter in re, suaviter in modo
[memento] coelum non animum mutant qui
trans mare currunt

Acknowledgements

Every book is like an empty canvas, a tapestry on which choices of subject, colour, style and aesthetic narrative are the choice of the artist. However, during the time in which the artist works and recreates the canvas or the page he is influenced by people, beauty, suffering and life that surround him. Thus, my acknowledgements are to those who have made this process of filling this particular canvas fruitful, painful, controversial and even personal.

This third volume has been inspired through many years by the great men and women who in times of uncertainty and confusion showed in a public way their discontent with militarism, violence, torture and false dreams of 'great nations' with 'small peoples'. Thus, those three Jesuits chosen for this book's dedication are only a symbol of thousands of others; their love, and their anger, has remained an inspiration for my ongoing commitment to intensity in my own recreation of social and personal realities through writing. Pepe Aldunate, a Chilean Jesuit, led those who, soaked with water and chocked with tear gas, learned the gentleness of God – I learned from them all; Dan Berrigan challenged an unlawful state and has given us the aesthetic beauty of jail and poetry together – I fear that I was too young and too broken when I could have followed his steps; John Dear has brought courage to Christianity in the twenty-first century and has systematized God's stand for peace in the world. Their inspiration has moved thousands to love God and his Kingdom in the midst of the periphery.

I am thankful to Professors Marcella Althaus-Reid and Alistair Kee, both based in Edinburgh, for their encouragement, support and ongoing friendship; to Dr Louise Lawrence for guiding me through the landscapes of Galilee, for commenting on issues raised in Chapter 2 and for her friendship, and to Gabriela Zúñiga for her own memories of desolation and hope over lunch in Santiago. I salute you Muriel Dockendorff; I wish I could have discussed this manuscript with you before the beasts took you away, *hasta la victoria siempre*!

I am grateful to Professor Philip Esler, Professor Ron Piper, Dr Ian Bradley, and Dr Eric Stoddart for encouraging this kind of research and for their friendship. I have discussed parts of this book with my doctoral students, that is, Dr Cheryl Wissmann, Dr David Wilhite, Dr David Brannan, Jennifer Kilps, Jeff Tippner, Rob Whiteman, Jonathan Rowe, Yumi Murayama, Casey Nicholson, Gordon Barclay, Alissa Jones Nelson and her husband Matt, and Joanne Wood; I thank all of them for their ideas and challenges. My family in St Andrews and Edinburgh has been always supportive and I thank Laurel and Sara for allowing writing to become a way of life rather than a part-time occupation.

Finally, a word of thanks to Barbara Laing, SCM Senior Commissioning Editor, for believing once again that an idea shared over an extended lunch could become an academic work.

Mario I. Aguilar
St Andrews, September 2007

Introduction

The Theological Irruption
of the Periphery

In volumes I and II of *The History and Politics of Latin American Theology*[1] I dealt with the genesis and development of a Latin American theology fit for the late twentieth century. The movement for justice and liberation originating with the underdogs of history after Vatican II created a furore, both positive and negative, in Europe and the United States, because it was a new challenge to the European centrality of a postcolonial theology, which in Catholic circles had been centralized in the theology of Karl Rahner and in Protestant circles centred in the modernist critique led by Karl Barth.[2] However, processes of European secularization and the critiques of modernity led to an emptying of the pews and a forced retreat by most of the European churches from the centre stage of politics, with the brief interval provided by the fall of the Berlin Wall, triggered as much by the decline of Soviet socialism as by the arising of a strong Catholic Church in Poland and the election of a Polish Pope, John Paul II, in 1978, a fierce critic of communism and of liberation theology.[3]

After Vatican II (1962–65) there was a change of theological climate triggered not only by the council's direct engagement with the contemporary world and secular society but also by the stress on 'the people of God' as an all-embracing concept and the affirmation given and deserved by human conscience within the relations of God, the Church and the world.[4] After Vatican II and with the visit by Pope Paul VI to Kampala (Uganda) and Medellín (Colombia) there was an ongoing support from Rome for the development of a Latin American Christianity as well as an African one.[5] The appointment of Cardinal Ratzinger (later Pope Benedict XVI) as prefect of the Congregation for the Doctrine of the Faith (CDF) started changing that theological spectrum of diversity and by the time that the Latin American bishops met in Santo Domingo in 1992 the Vatican theologians and advisors, among them the Chilean cardinals Jorge Medina and Francisco Javier Errázuriz, started taking centre stage and pushing for a return to a more middle-of-the-road orthodoxy without the orthopraxis previously advocated by liberation theologies.[6] The contextual theological narratives of liberation, of a gendered God and of a God who preferred the poor were pushed to the margins with the systematic appointment of more traditional bishops who had had a theological upbringing that corresponded with a more orthodox theological view or with no theological view at all.[7]

Towards the Twenty-First Century

In the two previous volumes I examined, described and assessed the impressive theological work of Latin American theologians within universities and pastoral work within the context of the military regimes and the Cold War. In this work I provide my own personal understanding of the possible developments of Latin American theology, its contexts, problems and hopes. I have previously explored the possibilities of a theological reflection 'from below', and for the purposes of this work I understand and do theology as praxis, thus following Gregory Baum's understanding:

Theology is a rational exercise that follows upon the option for the poor and searches for an understanding of God's revelation that discloses its redemptive and liberative power. Theology as praxis is historically rooted; since history changes, praxis theology must move forward, through the interaction of the cognitive and agapic dimensions of faith, in an effort to formulate God's revealed world of rescue and hope addressed to people in the present.[8]

In constructing this theology of the periphery, I follow the latest questions posed by Marcella Althaus-Reid and Iván Petrella.[9] Nevertheless, I ask questions related to a contemporary sociopolitical context, a locational questioning that complements those of Althaus-Reid and Petrella. Regarding my own experience of liberation processes and of Latin America, I make three clarifications in order to locate this work within a particular experience of Church and of the sociopolitical context:

1. my past and present experience of Church and liberation remains that of a theologian who believes in God and who has been all his life a practising Catholic;
2. my preferred choice of context has been the sociopolitical context within the peripheries of society, the peripheries of Latin America, the peripheries of the churches, the peripheries of globalization and even the peripheries within the so-called 'war on terror'; and
3. I make a distinction between political theology and a theology of the political in that I understand the theologian as immersed within the sociopolitical and particularly within the places where the poor of society live.[10]

Even when 'the poor' of Gutiérrez didn't have a personal face but looked more like a sociological group it is to the poor and the marginalized that one must turn in order to search for God, to experience the life of community and to construct local, contextual or liberation theologies.

Thus, this volume deals with the periphery as theological trope and as ecclesial construct starting from the dynamics of the periphery, Latin America, within a twentieth-century empire, that of the United States of America. The chronological time of this irruption of the periphery is the twenty-first century and the irruption has not achieved its maturity yet. The sociological facts are clear: the European decline in the practice of Christianity has led to a shift of Christian geographical practice to the United States and to Latin America where the majority of Christians in the world live and where large numbers of people still maintain that their identity and their actions are influenced by the gospel and by their belonging to many churches with many shapes, forms and traditions. Christianity as a globalized religion has shifted its centre and its periphery many times and this kairos is not the definitive one but a very central one because for the first time in the history of Christianity the centre of life and the theological centre for contextual theologies arising out of Christian communities is located in the Americas. As a result, the periphery of Europe has come of age because, as I would argue throughout this work, the periphery is the preferred locus for theology.

My perspective is of hope and optimism because it is at the periphery that God speaks to his people and it is at the periphery where everything started, there far away in the Galilee of the Gentiles, in the unexpected land of the uneducated Galileans, at the shores of the sea, not in Jerusalem, not at the centre of the Judean or Roman empires. Thus, at the start of the millennium the Argentinean theologian Marcella Althaus-Reid argued for the relocation of God in these words:

> The future of liberation and popular theologies may depend on this final understanding of the participation of the God at the margins with the projects of the centre. A truly 'marginal God' may have little common ground with the vicarious 'God of the poor' who, although visiting the margins, still lives far away and belongs to a central discourse of theology.[11]

Throughout this volume I take her challenge as a central theological presupposition and I expand on different areas that can be helpful to construct a theology of God at the margins as a fresh theological start for Latin American theology in the twenty-first century. I would argue that the margins as relocated centres have become the centre for God's action and for theological action and reflection by Latin American theologians, academic and otherwise, lay and ordained, men and women, straight or queer. It is at the margins where God has gone, not as a God at the margins but as a God of the margins, of the marginalized, of the oppressed, of the poor and of the theologians among the poor and even of those outside the Church. For, in the words of Willem Frijhoff, 'there is no more reason to be afraid of the flowering of the history of religion, of the history of faith and the Church outside of traditional church history'.[12]

Social Stories and Contrarieties

One of the persistent misunderstandings of Latin American theology vis-à-vis European theology is the importance of context and the tools of theological investigation and construction. This misunderstanding is unnecessary if one goes back to two of the great theologians of the twentieth century, Karl Barth and Karl Rahner. Both of them produced enormous numbers of writings about God and the Church within their particular contexts, both responding to particular theological challenges. If at the start of the twenty-first century their writings seem to be central to understanding the context of the Church in the contemporary world it is simply because their contemporary readers have forgotten that the two great Karls were theologians of their time. However, within times of war, postwar and secularism they managed to find theological answers to changing times, times that saw two of the greatest histories of suffering within a long history of humanity: the Shoah and the use of atomic bombs in Hiroshima and Nagasaki.

Contemporary theologians have seen enough films and read enough books about those two events to realize that those who commented on God and his plan within those two moments of great sadness and great annihilation took two different theological positions vis-à-vis God: (1) for some, God could not have been present in the extermination camps or in the howling cities of the undead and they could no longer believe in a loving God, could hardly believe in a God at all; (2) for others, the crucified God was in those situations and became one with the suffering in order to console and to redeem a crying humanity. European theologians would understand that those Latin American theologians who were labelled liberation theologians fall within camp 2, and that all they did was to try to accompany the poor, the oppressed and the suffering peoples of Latin America. Within that experience of walking with the marginalized they became part of the margins and their theological writings became closer to the Jesus of the Gospels, portrayed as walking with the marginalized, coming out of a marginalized area, and proclaiming values that didn't assure his disciples of any glories in a human kingdom but of a fellowship with those despised and rejected by the centre of society.

It is at this point that I want to stress the need to experience the social realities of suffering, poverty, hunger and oppression in order to understand why liberation theology arose out of the Church's experience in Latin America, Africa and Asia. Social stories from the margin need to accompany the theologizing because without those narratives, those texts about the poor and the marginalized, I would not be able to theologize. Therefore if Althaus-Reid argued that sexual stories and oral traditions about sexuality are central to the possibility of understanding and experiencing reality, I would argue the same in the context of the social marginality that concerns me, a sociopolitical marginality generally associated with exclusion from civil society rather than from the Church. In this theology of the periphery, the social margin the personal stories of peripheral life and the understanding of God as peripheral to the life of civil society are central to the theologizing because the first step in doing a theology of the periphery is the movement towards the periphery with the possible exclusion of the centre that was the Church and civil society in general. Using Nigel Rapport's expression of 'the contrarieties of Israel', meaning the possibility that social action contradicts principles and therefore that those contrarieties create social action by themselves,[13] I recognize that some of the social narratives of poverty and oppression could be contrary to gospel values as understood in traditional theology and that some of the actors and narrators follow patterns of social behaviour that contradict the norms agreed by society, politicians and ecclesiastical bodies. However, within those contrarieties and within those social scandals, usually situated in the periphery of organized and structured societies, there is one theological fact that remains and interests me: God lives there and has used people in the periphery as central actors within the Kingdom of God while rejecting the proud of heart, the wealthy and the rich, meaning those selfish enough not to empathize with any other human being and for whom there is never enough profit, enjoyment or investment.

A Peripheral Life

Throughout this volume I shall move between a diachronic and a synchronic perspective simply because without the diachronic it is impossible to understand some of the contemporary ways in which theologians write about God. Thus, even when I am located within Scotland writing about contemporary ways of engagement with God, with God's actions and about God, I have a history and a past that has influenced my way of doing theology and that has enriched my present and the theological reflections I have for the future.

I grew up in Chile, within a Catholic family of several political persuasions with enormous contrarieties – here is where this term is helpful because the dynamics of contradictions are very different from the term used by Rapport. Of course everybody in the family considered themselves Catholics until death but very few went regularly to Mass or confession. Everybody spoke highly about the stability of a long-term marriage. Only my grandparents managed to be together for 64 years, however, until my grandfather died in 1994. He had been a very devout Catholic in his younger years. When he got married, however, he decided not to go to Mass any longer as it seemed that my grandmother was not going to follow him to the Sunday Mass. All other members of my family, including my parents, separated from their spouses, re-married or discovered that they would prefer not to have a lasting and life-long relationship.

In this confused family existence there were conservatives and traditionalists like my grandfather, communists, socialists, Christian Democrats, people killed for political reasons and agnostics. However, one fact united all members of the family: the Church has a place and a role within society and that was to show mercy and love to the poor and those who had less than anybody else. With that point of view in mind, members of the family helped the poor financially if they were able to do so, others who were poorer adopted orphan children, others became priests and some joined the left-wing parties in order to paint poor schools and spend their weekends plotting the downfall of unjust socio-economic structures. The family provided a good education for all its members but it was peripheral to the centre of society because my grandparents were immigrants from the south of Chile to Santiago and there was no wealth, no titles of Spanish nobility, and no connections to the history of Chile or other parts of the world.

If I look back one fact stands out as central to that family diversity: every member longed to be at the periphery of things and perceived that God and fame were always present somewhere else. Those who became radicals, like my uncle, who spent six months in Antarctica, joined a leftist political party, built their houses away from urban centres, spent their weekends in shanty towns walking on mud and dirt and finally got expelled from the country or got killed. Even my grandmother who was a poet spent weekends with groups that lived within the periphery of society, being a poet rather than attending high teas with neighbours or friends. By the time that the summer holidays arrived a group would leave for the south of Chile, where relatives had farms, in order to live for one or two months without electricity or running water, sharing harvests and social events with poor farm tenants – those who didn't have land of their own and were allowed to live on a plot of land provided they worked for the landowner in return for the possibility of working a piece of land and growing their own vegetables.

I became a child of the periphery and, looking back on my

Introduction

life, I recognize that I have acquired that gene of longing to get away from the centre, a curious gene that brought me to the peripheries of Santiago, farms in the south of Chile, many areas of European urban centres where most people would not go, the north-east of Kenya and even to life in a shanty town in Nairobi, Kenya. More of this later. However, the point I am trying to make is that Latin American theology has come out of this kind of experience and that difficult years of political struggles and sharing the lives of those who are not significant for the international market economies or the financial institutions have created a theologian of the periphery because it is in those places where I have encountered and experienced the God of Life. Within the periphery the Church has been central to the life of people as have non-governmental and other community organizations in the daily struggle for food, education, health and a certain religious life informed by those religious and lay people who have lived and died as contemporary prophets of a life full of contrarieties.

Theological Arguments

In summary, my general argument is quite simple: Latin American theology has diversified its action and reflection, from the centrality of the Church as a political entity,[14] to the centrality of civil society,[15] to the ongoing awareness that a servant Church as proclaimed by the Second Vatican Council is always there supporting those Christians or non-Christians who are fighting for justice and who adhere, even unknowingly, to the values, attitudes and actions triggered by Jesus' proclamation of the Kingdom of God within a historical and sociopolitical context outside the control of the churches or their members. The periphery is the place where all of us should be leaving behind the dreams of greatness, self-importance and public recognition that many times are directly associated with the institutional churches and should not be part of a servant church, a prophetic and liberating church.

In my analysis my location as a Latin American theologian is clear. I was born and raised in Chile. I am and have always been a Roman Catholic, a practising Roman Catholic who finds his way through a daily engagement with the periphery, the periphery of prayer, of reflection and writing in order to support and encourage others who are deeply immersed in the direct implementation of the values of the Kingdom of God. I have always lived in the periphery, even with a Christian minority among Muslims in northern Kenya, and my theological thinking has been informed by the periphery within the traditional axiom 'action–reflection–action' following the theological dictum that considers theology as 'faith seeking understanding'. It is within the periphery, that is, in an underside of history, where Latin American theology flourishes. For as a result of the geographical distribution of practising Christians in the twenty-first century, Christian action and theological reflection are located at the periphery of society, but they are there, as they were after the 1968 Conference of Latin American bishops at Medellín, when committed Christians started rethinking their geographical location and left their places at the centre, flocking to the periphery in order to live together with the poor, the outcasts and the marginalized of society.[16]

A Contextual Theology

Two other approaches to Latin American theology for the twenty-first century have made an enormous contribution to the churches, academia and the political world in the past few years: the manifesto by Iván Petrella and the sexualization of theology by Marcella Althaus-Reid. Let me summarize again their central contribution to a diversification of Latin American theology in order to set out my theological position with its different sense of the sociopolitical context of a Latin American theology for the twenty-first century.

In his recent work Iván Petrella has dwelt on an important challenge – the Americas – and has argued consistently that:

Introduction

Today, liberation theology has abandoned the construction
of historical projects. This central element of early liberation
theology – indeed, the element which, according to liberation
theologians themselves, made their theology distinctive and
different from North Atlantic theology – lies forgotten, a
mere historical curiosity. Yet the development of historical
projects remains central to liberation theology . . .[17]

His location is Miami, a passage and bridge between North
America and Central and South America, and his writings saw
their genesis in Cambridge, Massachusetts. Therefore his writings reflect where he is and the challenge that he faces from
other quarters in the United States to resolve the tension
between his theological or religious existence, on the one hand,
and his identity as an Argentinean within a land in which
Latinos and Hispanics do exist, on the other. I chose this example in order not to solve a scholar's identity, mine is even more
complicated, but for the purpose of reflecting on the issue of
mixed temporalities, mixed identities and the complexities of
location, ideology, power and transcendence within the construction and ongoing authority of a theological construct, a
creed or a belief. Petrella's work emerges as a well-informed
and scholarly work in which he is looking for a historical
project within his critique of Latino and Black theologies that,
according to him, lack a materialistic side. His theology and his
writings on religion do not have a context and he is trying to
find one – a very contextual North American division between
the theology as canon explored in the seminaries and the objective and empirical study of religion by academic theologians in
their university faculties. Petrella's approach provides a good
way forward and a good contribution to discussions on liberation theology but ultimately lacks a historical project.

Marcella Althaus-Reid, a very prolific and elegant writer,
provided a surprise within the diversity of Latin American
theology: indecency. Her post-feminist approach to theology
stopped apologizing for dwelling on issues of gender or sexuality and incorporated all types of sexualities within a liberation

11

process that within her theology transcends the churches and academia. Her context is a social and emotional context usually ignored by Christian theology and even essentialized as alternative, peripheral and outside God's plan. Her theology has a clear context, that of Latin America, but not the Latin America that one usually hears about. However, her theology arising out of sexual mores and sexual actions in Argentina created a bridge, an important one, into the periphery. Instead of merely continuing a theological critique of patriarchy, she moved into the context outside patriarchy and produced a theology, a contextual theology, that speaks of ordinary lives and ordinary challenges by human beings who are sexed, who love and feel for others but sometimes outside the 'proper attitudes', attitudes determined by symbolic structures or the rules of a particular faith community. It is an exciting transgression within contemporary theology expressed in theological terms. She writes:

> Theologies do not need to have a teleology, or a system, yet they may be effective as long as they represent the resurrection of the excessive in our contexts, and a passion for organising the lusty transgressions of theological and political thought. The excessiveness of our hungry lives: our hunger for food, hunger for the touch of other bodies, for love and for God; a multitude of hungers never satisfied which grow and expand and put us into risky situations and challenge, like a carnival of the poor, the textbooks of the normalizers of life.[18]

Althaus-Reid has a clear context but less of a system and she deals very well with theories of the context without reaching into a postmodern agenda. Both Petrella and Althaus-Reid put together resemble the possibilities of a fruitful dialogue between fields identified as apart, for example, religious studies and theology, but that are mediated by the context and not by the ideology of the discussion.

For creeds and learned documents come out of social and

historical contexts and are adopted (and adapted by faith communities) with given understandings shared by all and others shared by most. If for Christians the kerygma is a common given, some of the later interpretations on ministry, church, authority, biblical canon, etc. are not symbolic realities fully shared by all Christians. For example, if all Christians within Latin America share a belief in the death and the resurrection of Christ they do not necessarily share the Eucharistic principles of some or the biblical centrality of others. It is within these parameters of theological and ecclesial diversity that my investigation of a theology of the periphery begins. The historical context always exists in front of us, in our midst, where we are, where we live and where a faith community interacts or avoids interaction with other communities, with civil society, with political and economic powers or the poor and the dispossessed of this world. There is no theology outside context as there is no proclamation of the kerygma outside a social context. My contribution hopefully complements those of Petrella and Althaus-Reid by assessing the same context in a different way – location, landscape and oral history.

The Contrarieties of God and the Theologian

I return to the theoretical model of 'contrarieties' of Nigel Rapport because one of the main criticisms of liberation theology was that it spoke about 'the poor' as a unified amorphous community without faces. Indeed, it was that way because without the possibility of bringing 'the poor' into Latin American theology we would have continued theologizing from above. There is a clear contradiction and many 'contrarieties' when it comes to understanding the primacy of a community, for example, 'the poor' and the individual, for example, God. Both of them seem to be interlocked and we would wish that they would understand each other perfectly so that theologizing would be an orderly process of understanding, a clear conception of inclusion and exclusion. That is not the case: not only do

'the poor' have their own agency and sometimes do things outside the Church and the Christian tradition, but God also plays
tricks as he remains labelled as 'the God of surprises'. Thus,
Rapport helps us to tease out these realities in the following
way:

> Construing the existence of 'words', of 'communities' and of
> 'individuals' can be seen as attempts symbolically to define,
> make singular, limited and congruous what is at the same
> time recognized to be multiple, unlimited and incoherent.

And further:

> For however 'mythical' the contradictions of the present
> order might seem, it is in fact ubiquitous. Both/and is a cogni-
> tive norm; it is the cognitive reality behind, as well as the
> creative source of, the everyday social reality of symbolic
> classifications of either/or.[19]

It follows that if communities such as 'the poor' seem to have
their own agency it is also possible for the theologian to expect
a God who cannot be controlled as an object of such theologizing. Both/and are possible and the location of God and the poor
could be the same. They could live in the same context that
could be located very far away from the traditional structures of
canon and tradition. If that were so, the location of the theologian seems of the essence for a process of theologizing because
if the theologian is not at the possible location of the both/and
there would be no theologizing about the presence of the God
of Life within a particular context.

The context then is where 'the poor' are located without
excluding the possibility that the contradiction between the
community and the individual can also exist in the same place,
in the same space, through the lens of the same landscape but
without any mediation between the both/and. I am suggesting
here that it is possible and quite plausible that God resides with
those who are at the periphery and that the margins are the

centre of God's world. After all the poor and marginalized seem to have been at the centre of the gospel message, not the temple, not the learned or those who already knew about the Messiah and didn't recognize him.

The axiom centre/periphery does not change as a category of divine representation but community/individual does. God lives at the centre, that is, the margins of society, but for the centre of structural religious practice that place is the periphery. This is where it is important to consider when theologizing the notions of community and the individual or both/and because God is a person who accompanies both communities and individuals. The challenge to Latin American theology is not only a locational one – to be at the centre of a divine presence which is the institutional periphery: it is also the challenge to interpret the social realities of the poor as individual realities of poverty, marginalization and annihilation. The social realities of marginalization that constitute the data or the prolegomena for theologizing relate to both/and, to the community and to the individual, both participants in a hermeneutical circle of marginalization/divine intervention/theologizing, both/and, so that theologizing = marginalization = divine intervention.

A Theology of Corpses

The construction of a theology of the peripheries follows a model of a Latin American contextual theology, keeping in mind that all theology is contextual, but that Europeans somehow have provided philosophical systems and ideas as theological paradigms. Those traditional theologies, by excluding other theological possibilities, according to Althaus-Reid: 'created the margins in the first place'.[20] It is a bodily theology because it is a theological reflection about bodies in movement, bodies in suspension, bodies in collision with others, and bodies that resemble corpses.[21] It is a theology centred at the borders of society, in the places not recognized as central to the institutions of governments or associated with a clean God and that are perceived as of no importance for the present or the future. The periphery is where the people without history, without a future and without a place in 'real society' live or die. In following that theological construction experience remains at the centre and a theological reflection provides the tools for a challenge to the centre. The main manifesto of this theology of the periphery is 'God lives at the periphery' not only because he chooses to be with those rejected by society but also because he is to be found within the history of the periphery, the history and the journey of the victims as outlined by Jon Sobrino, creating 'the *civilization of poverty* that brings humanization with it'.[22]

This is a radical theology for a radical age, a challenge to theology and a challenge to all of us theologians to return to the sources and to the early experience of Christianity, to remain among the pilgrim 12 of Galilee who with trepidation and fear, in the style of the hobbits of *The Lord of the Rings*, follow a teacher in Galilee to the periphery of the Roman Empire and to the peripheries of Rome, to the cross and to the resurrection, like the master. It is a post-radical orthodoxy because it is a call to return to early Christianity, to the Scriptures and to the narratives of the early martyrs rather than to the ideological fortresses of mediaeval times with their fear of the concrete and their fear of a possible assertion that all human beings are children of God, whatever the name or the community of that God. This is a twenty-first-century theology in which our own comforts and our own futures are at stake within a world that still strives for war, for mistrust and for material ecological destruction rather than stewardship of a planet that ultimately belongs to God. This is an unapologetic theology of discipleship as well as theological discussion but that centres any reflection and the doing of theology within all peripheries, all faiths and all those who according to Pedro Casaldáliga have not appeared in a TV reality show, have not scored a goal, and do not aspire to meet celebrities in order to be human.[23]

In the film *Romero* there is a scene that for years has touched my students: a young girl searches for scraps in the rubbish heaps that surround the city of El Salvador.[24] It is within those rubbish heaps that the Salvadorian dignitaries have to search for the body of a loved one, in the midst of the stench and the rubbish, in the midst of materials and people discarded by society; it is at the same rubbish heap that a young Salvadorian activist is tortured and shot dead, left with the rubbish of society; it is in that rubbish heap that Archbishop Oscar Romero found his conversion; it is there that Mother Teresa found God; it is there that St Alberto Hurtado of Chile met a beggar who made him into a Jesuit committed to social change; it is within that rubbish heap that God lives. It is within the social dirt and the rejected of society that God lives.

Thus, a Post-Radical Orthodox Theology is an interfaith and non-faith theology of service that worries less about the place of Christianity within society or about its centrality or de-centrality but worries about serving, about being, about helping create the conditions where through solidarity, affection and understanding the world created by God can become 'the world of God', a model closer to the servant Church rather than the teaching magisterial Church.[25] It is a theology that maintains the main Christian creeds as central to the life of those who consider themselves Christians but gives the same importance to other creeds, other faiths and other non-faiths, following Vatican II's centrality of conscience and its understanding 'the people of God' as an all-inclusive understanding of God's world.[26] No philosophical discussion about contra-modernity, contra-postmodernism or pro-scholasticism has a place here because those who are at the front of theology are those who cannot function in those terms and do not need to do so. They are part of a faith-seeking understanding whereby trained academic theologians can be part of that experience but they are not ex officio part of an experience of dirt because their daily context is of teaching not of doing, their ongoing preoccupations are secondary to those of the periphery where the present and future of society and of those who are Christians is being decided. I refer here to the manifesto of a Radical Orthodoxy by John Milbank and others because in his work on theology and the use of social theory Milbank has criticized the overuse of

Marxism by theologians of liberation; indeed, Milbank has overemphasized such use because Marxism is not the only base of a theology centred on praxis and certainly Gutiérrez and Dussel have used conciliar and ecclesiastical sources extensively in their works on liberation related to Bishop Bartolomé de Las Casas and the history of the Church in Latin America.[27]

This theology of the periphery is a theology of corpses and of bride-corpses because, as is the case in the film, even corpses have sociability, feelings and dreams.[28] The poor of the world resemble corpses; they do not count among the centres of power but as corpses they still have corpses' lives and they still have God. The manifesto of a theology of the periphery and of a theology of corpses is that God dwells among them and that God is one of them. God does not want people to live in poverty, as Gutiérrez has argued, but God lives among them so that, according to Gutiérrez:

> We should judge the premature and unjust deaths of the great majority of the inhabitants of our sub-continent in the light of this life that passes through death. Such a judgement will show us that what we call 'internal liberation' – a classic theme in the theology of liberation – means in the final analysis acceptance of the gift of the kingdom of life.[29]

The act of theologizing social – and Christian – experience comes out of a theological location vis-à-vis God, the God of the periphery by those who not only want to change the possibility of those theological margins being ignored but also provide a strong possibility of connecting the both/and through ordinary social connectivity, through the sharing of life and death, in order to become triumphant and joyful in life within the life of the God who doesn't want death but life. Within that social and Christian experience theologizing becomes a secondary act and the breaking of human and divine bread, within every group of people and within every Christian community, becomes the first act of life, solidarity and kingdom values so that, according to Gutiérrez:

The breaking of bread is at once the starting and the destination of the Christian community. In it we express deep communion. In it we express deep communion in human suffering – so often brought on by lack of bread – and recognise, in joy, the Risen Lord who gives life and raises the hopes of the people brought together by his actions and his word.[30]

It is in a particular context that theologians of the periphery find the both/and, the breaking of bread within the Christian community that is no more and no less than the ordinary breaking of bread of friends, family, neighbours, those who stand in solidarity and those who have decided to change their lives and move to the periphery in order to be closer to God. The breaking of bread not only relates to a metaphorical sense of religious ritual but also has been used as a sign of communion by many of those who have chosen the periphery years ago. Thus, at a gathering of Christian activists in Huddersfield in January 1973, Jim Forest and Dan Berrigan, after a ten-minute silence, distributed loaves of bread to all present while the charismatic Berrigan spoke in these words:

As in the communities where we come from, there are those upon whom the bombs are falling and those who are in camps or prisons and hospitals and are separated from their families and those they love, not by choice but by the iron will of war. Remembering them, we bless this bread and we eat this bread as the hope of men and women, that all may be fed.[31]

It is within those peripheral locations that become signifiers of hope, challenge and love that the context for theologizing is found and where the mapping of the Scriptures and the tradition help us understand location, landscape, identity and social connectivity. For God is in the social and the social is expressed by the Trinity and its both/and expression of love, the Holy Spirit, who brings peoples of all nations, all languages into a community of diversified breakers of bread and of those who ask questions about the missing bread, the missing link and the missing body.[32]

The Emerging Context(s)

The new emerging contexts for the periphery and the kinds of poor and marginalized who live and experience the both/and in Latin America at the start of the twenty-first century include: Mexicans outside the US wall, migrants and asylum seekers, slum dwellers, the victims of natural disasters (the product of global warming), the victims of economic disasters (the product of globalization), those who do not find a place in the churches, indigenous populations still hoping to be part of society, the landless, women raped by police abuse, children trafficked, drug-addicts, power-addicts, political prisoners, the unemployed, etc.

In order to highlight the both/and, the social and the individual narratives of the Latin American marginalized, it is necessary to problematize the either/or and to describe the context as social and individual, using sociopolitical analysis for an all-embracing narrative of oppression and structural sin while also listening to individual narratives that provide an individual context for the voices of the poor and the marginalized in the manner of life histories and autobiographical signifiers of social realities.[33] Within those personal and social histories there is an emerging sense of identity, and Jorge Larraín has convincingly argued that 'the phenomenon of exclusion as much as the phenomenon of solidarity has important effects on the process of identity construction in vast sectors of the Latin American population'.[34] In that sense the isolated context as social signifier provides a solidarity that can explain why those at the margins of society have created their own centres and their own divine paradigms of inclusion/exclusion. The avenues for a theological manifesto on the periphery could be manifold and my own choice of topics, themes and challenges follows Gutiérrez's 'irruption of the poor' and his sense of trying to mediate the pastoral with the social without forgetting that 'liberation theology has posited a distinction – adopted by Medellín in its "Document on Poverty" – among three notions of poverty: real poverty, as an *evil* (that is, as not desired by God); spiritual poverty, as *availability* to the will of the Lord; and *solidarity* with the poor, as well as with the situation they suffer'.[35]

Part 1

Contextual Issues

I

The Latin American Periphery

We exchanged the kiss of peace, with that strange Christian sense of joy which is so close to suffering, the blood of death and the bread of life shattering our nice categories. God's ways are not ours, his peace tears us to bits.[36]

Latin American theology in its strongest form, that of liberation theology, announced a new method of doing theology following a 'preferential option for the poor' so that Gutiérrez is very clear when he asserts that 'the poor occupy a central position in the reflection that we call the theology of liberation theology'.[37] Endless discussions following Gutiérrez's 'irruption of the poor' took place and he clearly restated what he was talking about, reiterating the three notions of poverty put forward by the Latin American bishops at Medellín in 1968, as outlined in the 'Document on Poverty': 'real poverty, as an *evil* (that is, as not desired by God); spiritual poverty, as *availability* to the will of the Lord; and *solidarity* with the poor, as well as with the situation they suffer'.[38]

Following on from Gutiérrez and exploring the location of the poor within contemporary society, I argue in this chapter that:

1. the sociopolitical and experiential exploration of the periphery constitutes the first step of a peripheral theologizing;
2. that the theologian is to find the centre of God's liberating action in the periphery; and
3. that the both/and of peripheral existence requires a tri-dimensional theological lens that proceeds from the periph-

ery to the nation state to the globalized community of a dysfunctional empire currently located in the North of the planet.

My methodology follows Gutiérrez's theological/pastoral paradigm by which experience and experiential knowledge of the periphery comes first, the theologizing second and the inscription of texts third, with an ongoing dialectic connection of destabilizing proportions between the context, the theologizing and the inscription of texts.

I am aware here of Juan Luis Segundo's problematizing of two types of liberation theology whereby for him liberation theology came out as a utopian challenge within the Latin American universities in the 1960s and 1970s and must always continue to be a written subject.[39] However, within Segundo's taxonomy of two kinds/types of liberation theology I follow Gutiérrez's paradigm of liberation theology (without excluding the possible validity of the other type/kind of theology) in that theology is a reflection on praxis (action) and orthodoxy a product of an ongoing orthopraxis so that, following Richard's synthesis: 'liberation theology is a critical, systematic reflection on the *experience of God* as that experience is lived, professed, and celebrated in a liberation practice. The object of liberation theology, then, as of all theology, is precisely God.'[40] The distinction between practice and praxis is also helpful here, so that 'practice refers to action in a particular sector of human life, such as educational practice, while praxis is made up of the entirety of human practices in the social realm'.[41]

Divine Surfing

'How do we find the periphery?' and 'Who lives in the periphery' are two different questions. We have already explored the latter within the lives and writings of Latin American theologians explored in volumes I and II. All of them found God while doing theology with the poor and the marginalized at the centre of their action–reflection–action and all of them systematized to some extent the praxis and reflection on God's liberating actions within the biblical text and within the communities, Christian and otherwise, located within the pastoral structures of the Church and the organizations and groups that constitute civil society in Latin America. Some of the theologians lived in the periphery but most of them experienced the periphery in an ongoing cyclical movement between centre–periphery–centre.

The question 'How do we find the periphery?' has a lot to do with a change of compass in which we reflect on our actions by exploring a cyclical movement between periphery–centre–periphery. I am here assuming that the majority of Christians are able to do theology (indeed they do it everyday when living their daily realities) and that most people live within a periphery of many other social, religious and political realities. However, I am also assuming that most of those theologians want to encounter God, want to experience God and want to live the Jesus experience as the Galilean 12 did (see next chapter). My presupposition is that the Jesus of the Gospels who later became the Christ of Faith showed a preference for the periphery and was born within the periphery.[42] Ronaldo Muñoz provides a theological reflection on this presupposition when he writes consistently and convincingly:

> Thus the one true God personally reveals an active presence and call not in the great ones of the earth, not in the 'sacred power' of human hierarchies, not in an elitist culture and the prestige of the 'governing classes', but *in our neighbour in need*, recognized and served as our brother or sister, and *in the multitude of poor and outcast*, with their privations, their misery, and their hope. God's dynamic presence and summons is not in the simulated order and cliquish security of a classist, repressive society, but in a longing and an effort for a more just and more human life and coexistence, along the path of love, solidarity, and the surrender of our very life.[43]

Imagine a God who surfs the waves of historical realities,

omniscient, wonderfully gifted, the God of the philosophical theologians, perfect in every attribute and having an all-embracing intellect, who knows all presuppositions, all post-propositions, all clauses and who can even upset the laws of probabilities while staying outside the truth/false and all Aristotelian propositions. That God suddenly chooses to live among the poor and the marginalized rather than be constrained by one kind of philosophical thinking. That all-knowing God knows more and better than any human and has to be part of many philosophical systems keeping the laws of non-contradiction alert and in place.

The both/and of context and theology can exist within the periphery if we find it. Some live in it throughout their lives and most probably find it very ordinary. Others are born within families that strive to own and control the world and whose God is clean, orderly and loves them. It happens that God loves all people but, in practice, those who do not mix religion and politics have a servant God who assures them that whatever they do is correct. Archbishop Romero, for example, disappointed many of the rich families in El Salvador even when most of them considered Monsignor as their friend, when he rejected the possibility of private baptisms, of resting and eating with them while the poor were starving. Further, Romero was highly disliked when he asked them if they were aware that their actions against people were not only unlawful but unchristian. Romero moved from the centre to the periphery but didn't create the periphery; the periphery was there to teach him. The case of Jon Sobrino is very similar: he didn't see anything until in 1977 he met Romero at Fr Rutilio Grande's funeral and he saw the realities of the periphery of Aguilares, outside San Salvador, outside the university and outside the safety of the Jesuit residence in the capital city. In the case of Ignacio Ellacuría, towards the later years of his life he spoke of being carried by the reality of the poor, by the poor and by people at the margins.

The finding of our own peripheries has a lot to do with finding the centre of God's action, the centre of God's revelation and the centre of ourselves; so that, according to Ronaldo Muñoz:

> We have to recognize the God of life, the liberator God, in 'signs of the Kingdom among the poor': solidarity, consciousness, commitment. This is the 'God of life and solidarity' who is present and active in 'organizations working for change', 'in those who give their lives for the people'.[44]

Muñoz is referring to people within the peripheral places in Santiago, Chile, and their own understanding of God and God's people because Muñoz has worked among the peripheral Christian communities of a difficult part of Santiago.

Webs at the Periphery

Those who already live within landscapes, urban communities, the countryside and the places where the poor and the marginalized live do not have to wonder how to find the periphery. I guess that there is a locational problem for those who live at the centre by choice, chance or fate. There is definitely a movement needed, be it geographical, personal, positional, ideological, theological or virtual – because so far no liberation theologian has had to deal with the internet and the possible relocation of a virtual theology of the poor.

After Vatican II and the Latin American bishops' Conference in Medellín in 1968 there was a movement to the periphery by pastoral agents, the religious, priests, political activists, artists, musicians and utopian dreamers searching as much for others as for themselves. In the early twenty-first century the media makes us believe that we are all relocating ourselves closer to the centres of consumerism, income and choice. Maybe that is true for some in Latin America but not for all – after all most Latin Americans do not have much choice but to live with relatives as they cannot afford a bank loan to buy their own house. However, the internet has provided not only the possibility of a surfing God but the possibility of virtual and mobile acquisitions of prestige and those values that Pablo Richard has called 'the idols of death'.[45] It is a reality that internet cafés have increased the possibility of idolatry and of a virtual reality full of power and prestige.

An example of this: whenever I visit Latin America, as I live in a permanent dislocation in Scotland, I rely on the internet cafés of the urban centres in order to check emails and disappear into the safety of a computer that I do not own but which I can check to see what God is doing in society and what I am suppose to be doing in the following hours, through pending appointments, conversations and trips into the periphery. All those movements remain dependent on an email by a peripheral citizen who has adapted to the contemporary mores and the contemporary challenges and who sends me a message about a possible subversive meeting. As I am given a computer by the attendant and after a long conversation about the fact that I speak Spanish so well but I am still not a native speaker, I notice two things. Most of those around me are younger than me and a significant number are using software to chat with others. The queer are all chatting, maybe constructing virtual theologies, near me. However, on one of those occasions I noticed one man who made me realize how the internet has provided the possibility of serving the idols of prestige, hopefully for a good, honest cause. He was sitting in front of a computer and his mobile phone rang. The conversation was quite formal and he intimated that he was in his office. Of course he could produce the document and fax it to his customer immediately. He ended his conversation, produced a CD-R, put it into the computer of the internet café and went to the attendant with two questions: could a file be printed for him and could the printout be faxed on his behalf? The answer was a 'yes' to both questions. He was dressed in suit and tie and went to the internet café to run his own personal office via a rented computer for most of the day.

How do we theologize about that moment in which a peripheral citizen with no job and no office has managed to become part of the centre of society in an urban centre? By arguing that at least God has brought hope to this person; maybe he would remain in the centre while I was trying to get public transport to go to the periphery. Nevertheless, that was human pretence at its best within the office hours of an urban city because together with thousands others the same man would return in the early evening to a periphery where his family or his lover would be waiting. This is the joy of the marginalized, to return to the neighbourhoods where they do not have to pretend any longer. Like the unemployed leftist intellectual who met me at the National Library in Santiago – 30 years ago we had been in the same cause and under the same oppression and community excitement. One of the greatest writers, university professor after his exile, he had lost his job under many cuts in a private university and still spent his day at the National Library sipping a coffee at lunchtime. After our afternoon coffee he disappeared into the masses that were returning to the periphery of the city – he was happy because he was bringing some bread and pasta for his wife and children. We promised to continue our conversation via email: we never did.

Social and Peripheral Texts

There are indications so far that an urban centre, a city for example, is divided between a centre and a periphery. 'Where do you live?' becomes a crucial question to divide those who belong to the centre and those who belong to the periphery. It is only at the centre that people ask the question 'Which school did you attend?' Because at the periphery schools do not have names, they have numbers, they are state schools that do not provide a movement within the centre, and they only fulfil the educational requirements imposed by a government.

The periphery does not exist within maps as expressions of inscribed reality, because the peripheries only sustain a social reality, a mass of people who struggle for daily subsistence and for a future. The churches are important because they provide a place of meeting, of social organization and of hope against hope. The bars are important because they provide a place to forget the daily realities, and sometimes within bars there are secret codes that could mean a temporary job, a helping hand or a future for one's children. The periphery as social landscape is painful for the centre. Thus, in the times of Pinochet walls were erected in Chile on the road from the airport to the city centre so that tourists would not see the slums and the large masses with their noise, their music, their folklore, their magic, their superstition and their underdevelopment.

Those pastoral agents, theologians, medical doctors, lawyers, freedom fighters and teachers who wanted more than consumerism and shopping malls crossed those walls and went to live and work at the periphery. As a result they became noisy and happy and their families were unable to understand why they went there. In my own family we had the case of a respectable university professor who moved his house to the periphery and spent weekends painting and repairing houses of the poor and the marginalized. He questioned his parent's way of life, the social injustices and his own Christianity – he didn't find religious answers after theologizing for six months in the Antarctica, so he joined a left-wing party and, after the military coup, he was killed.

The divine periphery attracts, consumes and asks it all; but it is there that one is stripped of any masks and any securities; it is there that the face of the God of Life shines liberating because it is there that there is more solidarity and humanity than anywhere else. The cases of Ernesto Ché Guevara and Camilo Torres are pertinent here: they came from well-to-do families and they asked questions about what they saw and experienced among the peoples of Argentina and Colombia. Great revolutionaries, great theologians and great saints have a lot in common, even when we try to block that reality.

Mapping the Periphery

As I have already argued, we find the periphery and therefore the context of theology within the periphery where the poor and the marginalized live. Even when Petrella suggested that the context could have changed I would argue that the political situations of the centre keep changing while the situation at the periphery remains constant because poverty and oppression are constancies within politics, within religion and within the parables and the sayings of Jesus in the Gospels. Indicators of poverty are not indicators of people's poverty; they are indicators that allow the centre to audit their own plans and achievements.

Therefore in mapping the periphery one must remember that general statistics are not what concern the God of Life or Juan or María within a slum of Santiago, or Lima or Bogotá. Their concern is to find food, health care, employment and human dignity. The maps of riches or poverty give indicators for public policies but they do not give hope, dignity or liberation to the poor and the marginalized. Here, again I disagree with Petrella when he argues that liberation theology has never engaged itself with economics. I know what he is saying – theologians work utopias without looking at the figures; this is to misunderstand the role of theology as a reflection on peoples' actions and the liberating actions of God within the periphery of society. However, there is a point in which Petrella is right: the need to inform ourselves as theologians on the reality of a globalized world, a nation state and a neighbourhood.

In mapping the periphery the theologian can take a map of a city (let's say Santiago) and the following questions can be asked: Where are the centres of government and the political institutions of this democracy? Where are the nicest neighbourhoods from which those who have nowhere to live and those who do not have work steal? Where are the shopping centres located within that map? For it is in those shopping centres that thousands of dollars are spent on items that are superfluous for a daily life. For if God can surf the web and google, theologians, pastoral agents, and indeed committed Christians can also google, surf and navigate a Google map that indicates where streets, locations and resources do exist or have been taken away. In the case of Santiago, the axis of East/West or Up/Down within the cartography of the city lies at a central point: the Italian Square (Plaza Italia). There is wealth and a good life spreading from the Italian Square up to the hills, where the numbers of new houses with swimming pools, security guards and 4x4 vehicles parked inside perimeter gates have been growing: that is not the periphery but the centre of economic power, even with more power than the elected politicians. It is there that prophetic theologians have been deemed communists and where General Augusto Pinochet arrived after his stay in the United Kingdom in order to have a full medical check-up at the Military Hospital.

Down from Italian Square there are centres of government and of the city, while further into the city centre there are thousands of empty buildings that were central to city life during the twentieth century and that remain unoccupied. On the way to the airport, along the Mapocho River, there are thousands of houses and many places, populated by those who sustain the life of the city but struggle with their own poverty. It is there that the traditional cemeteries are located, where there is night-life, cafés, brothels, where transvestites walk the streets and where it seems that the twentieth century has not arrived yet. Such areas are still peripheral to central Santiago and to the wealthy people of the hills. Those places are not slums. Crimes of passion are reported by the newspapers, the tango is danced in the Chilean way and the God of Life assumes a life of distance and of suffering. Instead, the Virgin Mary and the saints are present in that life of late nights and early mornings, replete with drunkards on the streets and the smell of rotten vegetables, unwashed clothes and romantic intensity. I never lived there. However, there are very flourishing communities and the example of Bishop Enrique Alvear remains as one of those who lived with them and took part in their sufferings.[46] The greatest Chilean theologians live in that northern pastoral area of

Santiago where time has stopped and where poverty exists but is fought by human solidarity, music and football played at a communal level on football fields denuded of grass, games played by those without fame and without a future.

To the south of Italian Square lies the southern pastoral area of Santiago (Zona Sur), the most difficult, the most violent, and the pastoral area that didn't give up under the military and where even the police on the day of the military coup of 1973 could not enter. Those who did enter La Legua on that day were killed and their bodies hanged from the trees. The repression that followed was enormous as was the poverty because in La Legua there is no employment, no decent housing, no good schools and no future. But it is there that the liveliest Christian communities and the most courageous priests and theologians live. It is there that the young inhale glue in order to forget and it is there that the God of Life has chosen, after careful surfing, to live. The map to be navigated is dangerous; people carry knives; strangers are not welcomed; and many are without jobs, without a future and without dignity – that is by the perceptions of traditional theology – and the centre of the periphery is located there. And it is there, in that marginality of inscribed social reality, in that embodiment of political failure and inequality that foreign missionaries and theologians found a genuine response to the values of the Kingdom and solidarity with others that surpasses the European imagination. And I lived there after my European theological education (more on this later).

This short exercise on theological mapping is only an example of what a theologian faces when writing about God and the processes of liberation because it is a challenge to all to recognize that the God of the periphery lives there and that the periphery has become the place where the God of Life has chosen to liberate and walk with his people. Local theologies and incarnational reflections have taken place there, outside the usual places of theologizing and within a location of destitution, crime, incest, drug-addiction and promiscuity. It is there where God has spoken to his people and has led them in many moments of confusion, oppression and poverty. This is not a utopian reading of the periphery but a chilling reminder that the Gospels and the social doctrine of the Church remind us that the best theology is done in the periphery and that salvation is daily offered to people who show communal solidarity rather than individual greed, people who at the end of the day do not count for the makers of the world financial centres and are only a statistic. If a people-centred God is active in the world through the Church, and many other means, it is possible to feel that activity within the people of the periphery rather than in any engagement with economics, be they local or globalized.

Theologians and Peripheries

Within the periphery there are many theologians, those involved in reflecting on the possibility of hope and liberation within different situations. The first theologians of the periphery are those who live there themselves: when faced with a glue-sniffing youth they do not ask about the person's sinfulness or for evidence of their acceptance of grace or about the absence of a grace-given event. They ask questions within their Christian community about what to do about a social problem – the sinful structure to which Medellín would refer – and what Jesus of Nazareth would have done himself regarding this social problem, as well as with the person himself. The role of professional theologians such as Ronaldo Muñoz, for example, has been to encourage members of the community to reflect on daily realities by reading the Bible knowing that since 1891 in Catholic circles the social doctrine of the Church has supported community involvement with social realities that are far from ideal in terms of human dignity. Muñoz's approach and location within urban slum communities is not unlike that of Juan Luis Segundo among his university and professional groups in Uruguay or those of Enrique Dussel or José Míguez Bonino in their own group dynamics and pedagogical initiatives with youth groups, ecumenical groups or groups of dialogue between Christians and Marxists, or Christians and atheists.

For each theologian the periphery remains centre stage for God's performance of grace on those who are marginalized geographically and socially. It is not the centre stage for the theologian's performance. It is God who chooses to save now and later, in this life and in the next. It is not the theologian who saves anybody. Elsa Támez concluded her seminal work on justification, Paul and grace by arguing that:

> Insofar as it is by faith and not by law that one is justified, the excluded person becomes aware of being a historical subject and not an object, either of the law or of a system that subjects her or him to marginalization. By being justified by faith in the one who raises the dead and brings to life that which does not exist, the excluded person is incorporated with power into a new logic.[47]

That 'new logic' challenges exclusion and marginalization at all levels, but particularly any marginalization as exclusion by theologians, be they those reflecting within the Christian communities or those writing theology for academic, scholarly or ecclesiastical purposes. Of course, this is a heavy responsibility for the ordained or academic theologian, who should have a deep sense of the need to support sinners and condemn the sinful structures and the creators and perpetrators of those structures.

If those theological demands coming out of the periphery apply to those who are living within the periphery the same search for an orthopraxis remains a task for the theologian who does not live within the periphery. Here it is important to note that after the 1968 meeting at Medellín and the implementation of many pastoral policies that had originated at Vatican II and were later reinforced by Medellín, many pastoral agents, members of religious orders and theologians moved from centres of power to the periphery; archbishops even sold their palaces in order to live a life in ordinary places where they could support and learn from neighbours and members of Christian communities. The examples are plentiful, that of Pedro Casaldáliga in

Brazil (see previous volume) or of Bishop Enrique Alvear of Chile, auxiliary bishop in the archdiocese of Santiago, who used to stay with families over weekends. Alvear arrived in a neighbourhood on a Friday, visited families and slept on any sofa or floor available in order to get to know neighbourhoods and to remain with a Christian community for a few days at a time without falling into the traditional formal occasion of a bishop's visit for confirmations and only for the administration of the sacraments.

If a theologian is longing to understand God then the theologian must experience the lives of ordinary people within the periphery. That is not always possible but I would compare the theologian's life with that of an anthropologist. If an anthropologist does not conduct participant observation and an extended period of fieldwork that anthropologist does not have any authority to write and research at the highest level. Following that example, I would argue that a theologian who does not live the life of the periphery at least during one extended period in his or her lifetime becomes a historian of dogma and a literary expert on the Bible rather than a theologian for, in the case of Latin America, a theologian must yearn for the periphery and must have an experience of what life is for the poor and the marginalized. Otherwise his theology will be no more than a reverberation of academic arguments for the consumption of the few. A theologian of the periphery is the one who is never satisfied with the acceptance of poverty and injustice and brings his or her own talents and tools to the support of a reflection on praxis from the point of view of the periphery, from the perspective of the poor and the marginalized, from the perspective of the excluded, even those who are excluded and discriminated against within the periphery and within the structures of the churches.

Examples of this longing for the periphery as theological reality are plentiful but three remain valid for theological reflection today because they had a lasting impact on the Church in Latin America and on the relations between Christians and atheists/agnostics within Latin American society: the worker priests, the

Sisters of Charity of Mother Teresa and the foreign missionaries who lived with the poor in the Latin American slums.

The case of the worker priests revolutionized priestly ministry in Latin America in the last thirty years of the twentieth century. It is assumed that Christian communities or religious congregations support financially the life and work of Catholic priests so as to free them to minister full time and be available to administer the sacraments throughout the year. However, the phenomenon of worker priests that originated in France in the 1940s became a challenge because it showed throughout Latin America that there were certain priests who wanted to move from a church-centred ministry to a way of life in which they were working as most people did within society, 'working in industry and living on their wages as workers'.[48]

In the same way, Mother Teresa of Calcutta responded to the call to send her sisters into Latin America and those communities quickly took up residence in the slums, with their usual personal generosity and commitment to the poor and carrying with them only a spare tunic and a copy of the Christian Scriptures. The same call to be with the poor and learn from them has been followed over the last 30 years at the time of writing by many foreign missionaries and communities who have settled in the slums in order to be part of the ordinary lives of the poor and marginalized.[49]

Subjects of the Periphery

The contemporary realities of Latin American peripheries remain centred upon the search for a fulfilment of basic human rights for all, taken for granted in the United States and Europe. The right to life remains threatened by unemployment within state systems in which there is very little provision for education or health and where people still die because they do not have money to go to a hospital and do not have money to pay doctors' fees, buy medicines or have medical checks done. Poverty within the Latin American peripheries is not a financial or economic indicator but it is a matter of life or death; human beings die because of poverty; and their human dignity as made in the image of God is crushed and destroyed. Within that social milieu Leonardo Boff has challenged the primacy of the individual and of private property, arguing that 'the common good is principally the good of the majority. It is the product of an option for the great, violated, oppressed masses. In theory and practice, democracy must begin with the marginalized'.[50]

Within the social realities of Latin America there is no state provision for housing or urban sanitation in many places so that people within slums have to face enormous health risks when winter arrives; thus, the image of a lively, sunny and happy Latin America sometimes portrayed by the media in Europe and the United States is not the full reality of life, and certainly tourists do not go the periphery and do not want to mix their fun time with the problems of others.

Thus, the theology of the political takes over political theology because the whole politics of society responds to the politics of the exclusion of the periphery, and discrimination takes place within and without society, within and without the periphery.[51] Any kind of discrimination and any kind of social rejection is evidence of oppression and therefore part of a theology of the periphery that liberates because God decides to liberate his people. The God of the periphery walks beside his people, each one of them, be they within or without the Church.

However, unlike processes of social charity where the poor and the marginalized are the passive recipients of aid and care, a theology of the periphery argues that the poor and the marginalized, those at the periphery, are central to the Kingdom of God and therefore become in their material poverty agents of change and agents of the Kingdom. God saves human beings through them because they challenge the possibility of a final acceptance of structural sin, of sinful structures as necessary and normal within society. The subjects of the periphery organize themselves so as to gather the sick, the unloved, the drug addicts, those with HIV-AIDS, the single mothers, the lonely, the alcoholics and those without a home in order to restore them to their human dignity. The agents of the periphery do not ask questions about sexual orientation, political affiliation, class, legal status, or personal ideas and welcome the excluded into the community of the periphery because God is the one who through them welcomes all. It is through this utopian sense of the human and the divine that there is a mediation between the holy and the unholy, between what is ritually pure and what is ritually impure, with the result that the Christian community of the periphery welcomes all, heals and accepts that broken bodies and broken souls need the periphery in order to understand that the love of God was shown by Jesus of Nazareth to those rejected and to the victims of society itself.

The Periphery of the Victims

I hope that it is becoming more and more clear that a theology of the periphery articulates the disjointed praxis of those rejected by society in a narrative of God's love for them and in a challenging discourse of not only personal care and empathy but also social and political challenges to those people and their structures that have created the possibility of a periphery of oppression and poverty. Today's victims of structural sin are the same as yesterday but the social, national and international processes that trigger those situations of oppression change their names and activities. If illegality and suffering were inflicted by military regimes, today processes of globalization and a war on terror create the same possibilities of arrest, torture and imprisonment in the name of social security. Prominent citizens living in the United States such as Ariel Dorfmann or Isabel Allende have been shocked by the security measures under the 'Patriot Act' and recently Allende has joined protestors against US Immigration and Customs raids at San Francisco Bay. Allende suffered a panic attack later that night, she said, 'because I realized that I had lived that before, with different nuances'.[52] If the victims of the 1980s were political opponents of the military, today they are indigenous peoples, protestors who challenge the historical injustice that deprived them of their lands, their language and culture; today they challenge the State that in the name of globalization and privatization has continued to negate their cultural existence within progress and development, within the need for profit and for multinational corporations to operate freely through a free-market economy that puts profit above human beings.

This theology of the periphery is a bodily theology and a theology of corpses because it highlights the social exclusion of Latin Americans from any globalized miracle, including that of Chile, 'the tiger of Latin America', meaning the tiger economy. Within 'the tiger' the victims do not share the spoils of the private companies or the justice given to the perpetrators of human rights abuses who live in luxurious jails when in custody and under the protection of the army when denying their crimes in the courts. However, one must resist the possibility that if the economic miracle were to happen a 'Gospel of prosperity' would be followed, because then the Christian prosperity would change once again the periphery for the empire, and Christianity for Christendom, following Pablo Richard's historical analysis of a gospel-centred decline in historical terms.[53] Nelly Richard, a Chilean cultural theorist, proposed even that the rising of postmodernism was helpful to Latin America because it would end the phenomenon of Euro-centrism; it would bring Latin American cultural paradigms out of the periphery. She poses the ongoing challenge as follows:

> Part of the challenge revolves around the conversion of the post-modern theme to a Latin American key, a project that raises the question of value, insurgent or resign, of the new relations of authority and cultural power between: Latin American marginality and the post-modern defence of the margins, the crisis of authority and the meta-narrative of the crisis, the theory of de-centring and the centre-function of this theory as a symbol of cultural prestige, and the rhetoric of difference and the politics of difference.[54]

The challenge does not take into account, as usual, the position of the poor and the marginalized but relates to a conversation without a social context in which Nelly Richard can speak face to face to North American and European partners in a language that is not that of the oppressed. Indeed, Hernán Vidal, involved in a historical materialist project of study of revolutionary and ecclesial movements in Latin America has been bold enough as to reject such a project, stating that 'I suspect that to discuss the profile of the forms of subjectivity generated within the unequal and combined development of dependent societies under the label of "post-modern sensitivity" is a theoretical diversion, an ideological trap, and a waste of time'.[55] Others have followed Nelly Richard's thought. Their position of analysis is not, however, that of the victims. It is a cultural relativism that allows for diversity but at the same time does not create a defence mechanism against imported ideas that in most Latin American cases are used to justify political policies that do not support a return to a discussion on modernism but replace modernism for post-modernism in an abrupt and semi-colonial manner, providing a recentralization of cultural identities outside the experience of the victims and within an avant-garde that systematizes autonomous models that do not account for Latin America's foreign debt or the violent rising of indigenous populations.

In terms of twenty-first century international relations there is one empire, currently the United States, and Latin America has ceased to be even 'the back water' or 'the back yard' of that imperial positioning, having been replaced by the Middle East and China. In my opinion, the position of Latin America while stronger in economic terms has become even more marginal than in the 1980s and even the global campaigns for alleviation of poverty have been centred in Africa rather than in Latin America. Despite that position of increasing marginality there has been a confrontation between the periphery and the empire in the words and actions of Venezuelan President Hugo Chávez who, by his criticism of empire, has not only antagonized President George W. Bush but also opened new avenues for a centrality of the periphery.[56] In his latest 'madness' Chávez has given free oil to other economic partners and has created a health service for Venezuelans, thus reducing dramatically the poverty indicators of that Latin American nation. Chávez, leader of one of the richest nations of the world in terms of oil reserves, has used his economic power to foster socialist governments and societies within Latin America and if he has antagonized the Church in Venezuela it is because the core of Venezuela's elite is highly connected with the Venezuelan Episcopal Conference and Venezuelan Catholicism has not been prominent within the social changes and challenges of Latin America in the last 30 years. Despite the fact that he was not able to dismantle an already planned project of electricity pylons throughout the indigenous territory of southeast Venezuela, Chávez triggered changes in the Venezuelan Constitution that gave further rights to the indigenous populations.[57]

I am not here suggesting that peripheral theologians should side with one political party, movement or personality rather than another, but I am suggesting that the historical location of religion and politics, the centre and the periphery after 9/11 have shifted context, action and social reality. I would go as far as to suggest that 9/11 becomes a marker of peripheral renewal, once again not because of its value as a nationalistic sign of victimization but as a sad moment of shift in globalization: from development and possible prosperity marked by international conferences on global disarmament and environmental protection during the 1990s to a war on terror, a violent and indiscriminate attack on the geographical peripheries of the world and the creation of legal limbos such as Guantánamo Bay as well as secret prisons and flights of attrition in the name of Western civilization and security connected with the nationalistic use of God for national interests and global violence.

It is within that globalized situation where Latin America remains a peripherical partner of North America and the European Union and a province of the Empire of the North with its economic power and multinational free trade agreements that an exploration of Galilee as a province of Palestine and of Judea as a province of the Roman Empire within the biblical text could give us further insights into the movements of Jesus of Nazareth and his disciples in and out of the periphery. This is the subject of the next chapter.

2

The Galilean Periphery

One of the challenges posed by Latin American theologians was to read the biblical text and particularly the Gospels within a contextual framework.[58] Within that complex hermeneutics of the text Gilberto da Silva Gorgulho has outlined two aspects of the use and reading of the biblical text that seem to encompass the general efforts for a Latin American hermeneutics:

1. the Bible is read in a popular way with the hermeneutic challenges of experience rather than academic knowledge; and
2. biblical hermeneutics becomes 'the interpretation of the praxis of liberation of the poor by Jesus of Nazareth'.[59]

That reading of the Bible is not neutral as claimed by academic circles because 'in the base communities, the poor do not approach the Bible as a source of erudition. They seek a *source of life*, of hope, and of perseverance.'[60] However, as pointed out by Carlos Mesters:

> We find three elements in the common people's interpretation of the Bible: the Bible itself, the community, and reality (i.e., the real-life situation of the people and the surrounding world). With these three elements they seek to hear what the word of God is saying. And for them the word of God is not just the Bible. The word of God is within reality and it can be discovered there with the help of the Bible.[61]

For Mesters this Latin American hermeneutical process goes back to the patristic method of interpretation so that the main task is not to interpret the biblical text but to interpret life with the help of the Bible.[62] Within that return to a biblical hermeneutics of life the preference for the Exodus narrative and the possibility of actual physical, social and political liberation has dominated much Latin American biblical hermeneutics to the point that the historical liberation of the past and the violence/oppression against the victims of today seems to pose a contradictory state of affairs. Within that contradiction the events of the past within the biblical narrative need for some such as Jung Mo Sung to be interpreted in the light of a crucified God, or in the light of a loving God who disorders history in order to sustain love rather than sin.[63] Further, Althaus-Reid has argued that 'the Latin American cultural inter-text from which the Bible (or the cross, in this case) is read is made, contrary to the belief of the liberationists, not from an experience of exodus but from an experience of Canaan'.[64] It must be remembered here that the context in which biblical reflections or hermeneutical explorations took place in Latin America when liberation theology started to challenge the social establishment was a period in which, for example, it was subversive to read the Latin American Bible, a translation with notes relevant to Latin America originally published in Chile: thus that biblical edition was considered 'an indecent book'.[65] It followed that the reading of the biblical text when trying to understand the context and the history of Jesus of Nazareth became a subversive act and a challenge to the established order because it provided new ideas for the readers about the centrality of the values, attitudes and socio-ethical system associated with Jesus' proclamation of the Kingdom of God.[66]

Following from that subversive and transgressive hermeneutics of praxis, this chapter explores the Galilean periphery of the biblical text or, better expressed, it explores the journey by Jesus of Nazareth and his disciples from the periphery to the centre, from Galilee to Jerusalem, from youthfulness to maturity, from first preaching to death, from oppression to full liberation, from citizenship to martyrdom, from the province to the ritual and imperial centre of Jerusalem. I have chosen to follow Jesus' journey within the Gospel of Mark for no obvious reason than that it is the shortest and therefore the first one to be read by Christian communities in Latin America. Within that reading I shall call Jesus' disciples the Galilean 12 because all of them were challenged by the journey; I shall use the trope of periphery in order to look for markers of landscape, of choice, of identity within the journey of Jesus of Nazareth knowing that the first reading of every Christian focuses less on the Chalcedonic image of Christ and more on the human person who has accepted a call and leads a group of followers into 'the belly of the beast', into Jerusalem where the leaders of the Jewish people, the Jewish temple and the Roman governor interact within a religio-political game of colonialism, imperial and local politics.

This reading evokes the possibility of reading in community because my community at this stage in life are the readers of this work. I am solely pointing to my own liberating process of understanding God's work within Latin America today so that readers may understand that one of the aims of this contextual reading is to make the text familiar within human situations comparable to those in which we are involved. Thus, in the case of the Christian communities of Latin America Faustino Teixeira has pointed to three elements that arise out of a familiarity with the biblical text: '*involvement* in and *commitment* to the world of the impoverished and *closeness* to the Lord of history'.[67]

The Dialogic Periphery

Current biblical scholarship has pointed to the possibility that Galilee has been romanticized as the countryside of any nation could be romanticized. Nevertheless, the identification of Jesus with Galilee as a Galilean strangely enough appears only once within the Gospels and in the context of Jesus' trial in Jerusalem (Mt. 26.69). Others such as Peter are asked if they are Galileans in the context of being in trouble. Thus, the maidservant asked Peter if he was also a Galilean because of his accent (Mk 14.70,

cf. Lk 22.59). In John's Gospel the Pharisees asked Nicodemus
if he was a Galilean because he was trying to defend a new interpretation of the Law by Jesus (Jn 7.45–52).[68] Despite those few
associations between Jesus and Galilee, the fact that Galilee was
at the periphery was important for scholars in their attempts to
understand the historical Jesus in his sociohistorical context
and the fact that Galilee was a very creatively mixed location
for Jews, Hellenists and all sorts of popular movements that
contradicted, if not challenged, the understanding of the Torah
by the rabbinical teachers and scholars in Jerusalem.[69]
However, Sean Freyne has asserted that 'For Mark, Galilee is
the place of definitive disclosure of the meaning of Jesus as
God's agent of salvation' so that:

> Galilee is charged with a highly positive symbolism in terms
> of the proclamation of the early church concerning God's
> saving action in Jesus. As such, it stands over against
> Jerusalem, the holy city, whose central role for Jewish hopes
> is recognised, but which tragically remained unfulfilled
> because of the rejection of Jesus.[70]

Despite those definitive words, locations, maps and reading
of maps show contradictions not because social agents fill them
with their own details but because in the case of texts we are
dealing with the difficulties of the positioning of readers and
writers vis-à-vis a text in what Bakhtin has termed 'the dialogic
imagination'.[71] It is within that imagination that dialogism
becomes the possibility of opening a particular location as a
giver not of meanings but of celebratory modes of liberation. It
is within that carnival, that Galilean carnival rather than the
Bakhtinean idea of the carnival as *heteroglossia*, limited but
open to changes, in that the poor and the marginalized evoke
social passions and social dreams.[72] Thus, the reading of the
journey in a somehow contemporary text, assumed as canonical in Mark's Gospel, reflects the contemporary possibility of a
closed text, and we all prefer closed texts, but a text that was
open for the author and open for the many Christian communi-

ties that have read it throughout the ages; in fact, 'there is no algorithm of history' and 'change bespeaks *heteroglossia*, the unsystematic conflict of tongues'.[73] For there is a more open way through 'dialogism', assuming that author and reader also navigate, together with the canonical theologian, a textual landscape that has no fixed meaning. In the words of Michael Holquist:

> Dialogism argues that all meaning is relative in the sense that it comes about only as a result of the relation between two bodies occupying *simultaneous but different* space, where bodies may be thought of as ranging from the immediacy of our physical bodies, to political bodies and to bodies of ideas in general (ideologies).[74]

I cannot avoid thinking of the Hobbits in the *Lord of the Rings* who leave the Shire full of dreams, without fear, without imagining what would happen to them. When the Galilean 12 left Galilee, they must have felt an excitement similar to that experienced by the poor and marginalized. They were able to visit places without assuming that Jesus was fully aware of what was going to happen next, and have had understanding of what the Kingdom's promise to the poor and the marginalized meant.

Whereas Bakhtin allowed readers to concentrate on the possibility that there were different locations and open texts, the periphery has been 'inscribed' within Paul Ricouer's assumptions of text as social action because a text has in it symbolic utterances that provide readers with a sense of what has been happening and readers can reinvent those social actions within their own sociability.[75] In allowing a textual periphery to speak to us we are allowing a process of literary, human and divine liberation, in which the Gospels are central to the life of Christians but the words as text need to be negotiated within an ongoing hermeneutics of suspicion, allowing for the fact that canon, biblical and theological, took some time to be constituted. However, within that 'dialogism' I take very seriously R. S. Sugirtharajah's criticism of liberation theology and its solely

Christian hermeneutics when he suggests that 'the dominant presence of liberation theology has tended to overshadow and conceal context-sensitive vernacular texts, and has also silenced the pioneering and often daring efforts of an earlier generation of theologians'.[76]

The intention of Mark the writer was certainly to inscribe in the sense of Ricouer the social action that has been conveyed through stories by those who in Jerusalem and in Rome remembered what happened to the Galilean 12 when they journeyed to Jerusalem. Mark's Gospel has been certainly crucial in the lives of many Christians who have looked at it through the eyes of a possible road to discipleship. As Richard Horsley has indicated, however, such a reading has a lot to do with modern Western individualism because 'those who interpret Mark along this line, however, must do mental gymnastics in order to explain the Gospel's increasing negative portrayal of the twelve disciples'.[77] Indeed, the disciples are called to join Jesus in his ministry of healing, exorcism and community but they fail to understand him, and in real terms Jesus has to continue a journey through the countryside and to Jerusalem with a group of companions who seem not to be of much help apart from their companionship and, one would expect, friendship.

In the following materialistic reading of the Gospel of Mark I am indebted to earlier works such as those by Fernando Belo and Michel Clevenot's continuation of Belo's work in which literary criticisms and Marxism as tools for biblical hermeneutics were used.[78] However, if at the time of the publication of Belo's seminal work these approaches were new by now they have been assumed within the possibilities of a rapid and varied development of biblical hermeneutics marked by the socio-scientific approaches to the study of the biblical text and the literary contributions from social anthropology and literary criticism. If Belo expanded on conflict within Mark, and the central place of the preaching in Jerusalem occupied a central point within that system of conflict, I prefer to follow a materialistic reading with Galilee as the centre of the periphery because it is there that the disengagement with the central normative narratives of Judaic purity/impurity and social inclusion/exclusion take place; in other words, the view from the periphery prevails within a diachronic reading of Mark's Gospel in the historical developments that would connect Galilee with Rome as peripheries for the disciples of the Jesus movement, expanded by the Galilean 12 once they leave the centrality of Judaism as their terrain of kingdom expansion and expand their teaching and communities throughout the Roman Empire and Asia Minor.

Shaping the Periphery

At the beginning of the text of Mark's Gospel John the Baptist's proclamation of a baptism of repentance, of a change of life, announces the possibility that people within the periphery and not only within the Jerusalem temple could have access to purity (Mk 1.1–8). The baptism in water resembled the practices of the Essenes, those who had fled the world in order to live a purer life in the desert. Indeed, John the Baptist lived in the desert, at the periphery of things, and Jesus after his own baptism at the River Jordan spent time in the desert (Mk 1.9–13).

In starting his ministry, or what we understand today as his ministry, Jesus started to encounter misunderstanding because of his social attitudes of inclusion that provided a challenge to the established social manners of engagement of that time. It is here that the myth of the particularly depoliticized Jesus as the Christ of Faith must be confronted because Jesus as a religious figure with no social crises and a model for a personal salvation without politics has very little to do with the Jesus of the Gospels. The coincidences between a Jesus who ministers within a province of the Roman Empire and the Latin American poor and oppressed who must protest against economic and social policies from other empires, if not from one singular empire, particularly after 9/11, is extremely poignant. In his insightful 2001 Rauschenbusch Lectures Richard Horsley stated this connection in the following terms:

The 'coincidental' historical analysis is too disquieting, that is, that the Roman Empire had come to control the ancient Middle East, including Galilee and Judea, where Jesus operated. We have come to recognize that the ancient Palestinian people responded to Roman rule in a lengthy series of protests and movements. It is difficult to continue to imagine that Jesus was the only figure unaffected by his people's subjection to the Roman imperial order. If nothing else, then perhaps the fact that he was crucified, a form of execution used by the Romans to intimidate provincial rebels, should lead us to take another look.[79]

Following from that convincing argument it is possible to argue that the preferred characteristic of Jesus is his tableship with sinners whereby he did not feel constrained by ritual prohibitions or was not afraid of appearing not as a respectable teacher but instead chose to be known as somebody in touch with the periphery of ritual systems, because ritual systems include on the one hand those initiated into a particular symbolic community and on the other hand social/ritual exclusion for those who are not part of a community and even more for those who are not deemed acceptable or pure enough as to be part of a community. Jesus as teacher, as a venerable figure exuding divine teachings and high ideas does not belong either in Mark's portrait nor in a materialistic reading of a literary text. Thus Marcus Borg has cleverly commented:

> The authority of the teaching depends upon its own perspicacity rather than upon some external authority. Frequently sages use analogies drawn from nature or common human experience to illustrate what they are seeking to communicate, thus inviting their hearers to see things a certain way rather than insisting that tradition or revelation dictates a particular way of seeing things.[80]

The central texts within Mark and those who have created more discussions and more theologizing within Latin American

Christian communities and taken from Mark's Gospel have been the 'tribute to Caesar' and the pericopes related to Jesus' mixing with women, prostitutes and those who were unclean. Social inclusion is of the essence within a Latin American sociability. Therefore those passages are the most crucial ones; instead, in an African context Christian communities have a particular interest in those passages related to the nature miracles, exorcisms and the world of the spirits in general. I shall return to these passages later. However, Jesus' ministry in Galilee started with his proclamation of the Kingdom of God: 'The time has come', he said 'and the kingdom of God is close at hand. Repent, and believe the Good News' (Mk 1.14–15 [JB]). His calling of the first four disciples follows (Mk 1: 16–20) and immediately his preaching in Capernaum is followed by the cure of a demoniac (Mk 1.21–8), the cure of Simon's mother-in-law (Mk 1.29–31) and a number of further cures (Mk 1.32–4). In preaching further in Galilee he cures a leper (Mk 1.40–5) and a paralytic (Mk 2.1–12) while calling Levi to be his disciple (Mk 2.13–14).

Itinerant preachers do not provoke scandals or controversies; they exist even today in all urban centres of Latin America and they preach while people eat their lunch or walk down the pedestrian areas of central Santiago. However, then as today, society and faith communities have respected ritual purity as something central to the actual identity of a member of a community. Jews and Muslims do not eat pork, Catholics do not eat meat on Fridays or in Lent, all believers fast at one point or another, they cleanse their hands up to the elbows before the five daily prescribed times of prayer in Islam and those who break these rules of purity are considered unclean and outsiders to the community. Within that general understanding of all systems of religion Jesus sat with tax collectors and sinners together with his disciples and he was questioned for the first time by a party of Pharisees who were also eating together (Mk 2.15–17). Further, he was questioned about fasting because unlike the Pharisees and John's disciples he was not perceived as keeping the fast required by the rules of ritual purity within

Judaism (Mk 2.18–22) and Jesus was later questioned on the practice of his Galilean 12, when walking through the fields on the Sabbath, in picking ears of corn to eat (Mk 2.23–8).

A picture of a preacher who is following rules different from those of the establishment starts to appear. I must clarify that I am more interested in the act of transgression than in explaining the rules that made those actions transgressive. A reader within a Christian community in Latin America would perceive a social disagreement between Jesus and the Pharisees and the possibility that Jesus as a preacher was talking to people considered sinners rather than keeping to himself and talking to his friends. Is it possible to accept the sinner or is it necessary to reject sinners in order to aid their full conversion? Similar questions resounded centuries later when Augustine and the Donatists clashed on the possibility of appointing bishops in Northern Africa who had not resisted the Roman persecution; thus Donatists and early Christian monks fled from mainstream Roman-dominated Christianity in order to welcome theological diversity, thus including different kinds of Christian practice, while rejecting those who did not repent and change their ways of life.[81]

Jesus' ministry continued after that first ritual controversy with the healing of a man with a withered hand within a synagogue (Mk 3.1–6) and the appearance of crowds following him 'for he had cured so many that all who were afflicted in any way were crowding forward to touch him' (Mk 3.10). It is here that the relation between Latin American popular religiosity and liberation theology could clash because popular religiosity may continue to exist within the ritual periphery but does not always provide liberation. Popular religiosity is an expression of a clear exchange between master and servant, between feudal lord and *inquilino* (tenant), because in the case of a pilgrim who reaches a Marian shrine on his knees he, like a tenant, is offering some kind of physical suffering to his master, in exchange for a favour that usually involves a physical cure or a better fortune.[82] The pilgrim requires protection through a mechanical process of cause and effect within grace. Thus, this exchange between a human being and a protector God becomes problematic for the conception of a liberating God who offers grace as a free gift to the sinner without promises of personal prosperity but of a close life within the cross/resurrection paradigm so that according to Elsa Tamez, 'God transforms God's creatures because it is God's will that they should live with dignity their own history in communion and solidarity with God and with one another'.[83]

We can only guess what Jesus' intentions were, because the biblical text is silent on the subject, but his growing popularity led to the appointment of the Galilean 12 as apostles (Mk 3.13–19). Jesus' relatives were concerned, as most families within Latin America are concerned about their sons and daughters who join movements that are not part of the establishment or announce that their sexuality is not the one expected or that they are going to be poets, artists, actors or revolutionaries. His family cannot get him out of the crowd, however, and the fact that the scribes had come from Jerusalem suggest that he was already under investigation (Mk 3.22–30). Jesus' extended family tried again to come closer to him and he asserted that his family were actually those who were partaking of his ordinary life and that there was a family above that of kinship (Mk 3.31–5). Those who have decided to join a movement, be it revolutionary or otherwise, have experienced this separation from family, an ongoing process of ageing and maturing that requires leaving the centre of society and the negation of kinship while emphasizing a particular commitment to a mission perceived as a higher ideal. I can only think of those young Chileans who went underground after the 1973 military coup in order to reorganize the people as resistance and who were not able to see their families because their actual family were the underground revolutionaries with false identities under constant danger from the security forces. Althaus-Reid has described those processes of resistance, Christian or otherwise, as 'theological acts of disturbance that are also acts of collective love . . . those acts of love are acts of subverting, transgressive kind of love'.[84]

In any case and within Mark's text the Galilean periphery has already been shaped by Jesus' presence and ministry, his close attitude towards sinners, those possessed and those ritually impure and by his preaching of the Kingdom of God and its challenging values for society at that time – and today. The use of parables as vehicles of communication provided direct teaching to the crowds while the teaching was explained to his disciples in the inner sanctum of evening chats and common friendship (Mk 4, particularly 4.33–4). For those who were not part of the inner circle the parables were not explained because parables like jokes open a possible application of social realities and human relations but cannot be explained. However, the parables have been a central theme used by Latin American theologians and the so-called 'parables of today' have been very much part of the reading and reflection on life by the Christian communities associated with movements of liberation.[85]

The confrontation was not imminent but took place, not as a power struggle but as the challenge of a preaching that mobilized crowds at a time when the Jewish authorities were conscious that any public revolt would trigger a violent response by the Romans and the possible destruction of Jewish institutions and the temple in Jerusalem. The calming of the storm and the nature miracles can only be understood as moments in which Jesus' authority was shown and one would presume that within the text they accompany his teaching and his healings in order to point to divine authority (the messianic secret) as well as the capability of challenging socially unjust structures within Galilean society (Mk 4.35–41). Further cures follow until Jesus visited Nazareth where he encountered disbelief towards his preaching (Mk 6.1–6). It is at this point in the text that the mission of the Galilean 12 was to preach through a simple life and to cure those who were sick.

Throughout the following chapters Mark recalled the disagreements with the Pharisees about cleanness and uncleanness and Jesus' excursions outside Galilee to Tyre and Sidon (Mk 7.24–37). Peter's profession of faith remains at the centre of the text (Mk 8.27–30) and the passage has been connected with the development of the church in Rome and the future development of the petrine office, particularly within the Catholic Church. However, the passage that follows shows a different Peter, rebuking Jesus and his mission to Jerusalem, to the effect that Jesus compared Peter with Satan (Mk 8.31–3). The lessons given by Jesus in the following sections alert the disciples about the danger of riches and of power so that a child is greater than others (Mk 9.33–7) and those who follow Jesus must be ready to give up all their possessions (Mk 10.17–22), a requirement for those who want to follow but a reminder to all: 'How hard it is for those who have riches to enter the kingdom of God!' (Mk 10.23). This statement prepares the centrality of the Jerusalem ministry in which statements follow the central commandment of love of God and love of neighbour (Mk 12.28–34).

The Tribute to Caesar

For most commentators and certainly for Latin American theologians the central crescendo and climax of Mark's Gospel is the crucifixion, the empty tomb and the appearances. Indeed, Sobrino's work on the victims of oppression remains a masterpiece of diachronic interpretation and a marker of oppression/liberation vis-à-vis Jesus' crucifixion, death and resurrection.[86] However, if one were to treat Mark's Gospel as subversive and as political theology that pointed to the end of a challenge to Rome by a teacher who went too far the text constitutes one more moment in the long history of humanity, not the centre of that life and history. Thus, crucifixion and resurrection become central to the passage of the Jesus of history into the Christ of faith vis-à-vis the councils, decrees and doctrines that followed centuries later. For me the central moment of discourse for a teacher and those who deny him his freedom of speech is when he is asked to declare, honestly declare, his own opinions and to argue for them regardless of the consequences. The cases of Leonardo Boff and Jon Sobrino are pertinent here; regardless of their silencing or their contestation by Cardinal Ratzinger they could not change their mind in what they had written or interpreted within their theological texts. They could only be silenced because what was said could not be changed.

In the passage related to the tribute to Caesar (Mk 12.13–17) the Pharisees and the Herodians came to Jesus and after asserting that he was an honest man not afraid of anyone they asked him: 'Is it permissible to pay taxes to Caesar or not? Should we pay, yes or no?' Taking a coin of that period Jesus responded, 'Give back to Caesar what belongs to Caesar – and to God what belongs to God.'[87] I have written a longer commentary on this passage elsewhere. At this stage, however, it suffices to say that this passage becomes central to any understanding of the relation between centre and periphery within Mark's Gospel because it relates to a confrontation between religion and politics in which the consequences of Jesus' answer would either legitimize the oppressors or could antagonize them by challenging the payment of taxes to the Roman governor.[88] Those who have separated the social realities of religion and politics have used this passage or a misinterpretation of it as justification of their attitudes. The dialectic of the question and of the answer points to a response by Jesus that takes the answer out of the two given possibilities, does not deny the centrality of religion and politics but points to those reading Mark's Gospel to other values, other attitudes and other lives that have nothing to do with the centrality of government or religious organizations but with the Kingdom of God, that Kingdom already preached to the sinners and the marginalized that is not at the centre but within the periphery of the Jewish religion and of the Roman state. Indeed, for Carlos Bravo it is clear that 'the travesty the religious leaders make of God and his project is the principal obstacle to the people's hope'.[89]

Social memories, as outlined in the story of the 'tribute', are fragments of social existence, which continue to bring to mind human experience, and that in the case of areas such as religion and politics show an inconsistency that speaks of cultural and contextual constraints and contradictions. Even if Jesus disagreed with such taxation he was forced to pay it and therefore his divine plans and messianic statements were dependent on political events that were shaping not only his mission but the challenges of his opponents and the understanding of his hearers. On the one hand, studies of oral history suggest that people are capable of passing on stories and important memories; on the other hand, those memories are contextually recreated within a setting that cannot be the original one.

It is within such reframing of context that the 'tribute' appears contradictory and Jesus is perceived as a clever respondent to social challengers. His contextual setting is clear – a man who was a Jew and who believed in a God who was above emperors and kings, who had made a covenant with a particular people and who had established some law and order as well as an institutional framework to that covenant through royal dynasties, divine laws and sacred spaces. Any of those Jewish perceptions could not be compromised, however, as happened with Josephus – either the colonial subject cooperated with the colonial power or it was in trouble. Jesus' appeal within the 'tribute' is that he is able to live within two contested powers by suggesting that there are other social realities within a Kingdom that is not of this world, and in which neither Rome nor Jerusalem would be the leaders, but his Father.

Mimetic Condemnation

The rest of Mark's Gospel is solely a continuation of a dialectical conversation between centre and periphery. The centre represented by the state authorities (Roman and Jewish) and the religious authorities want to know if Jesus is challenging them while Jesus continues his march to Jerusalem in order to proclaim a Kingdom, that of his Father, that is not of this world and that, within the world of materiality, sociability and conviviality, is present within the world of outcasts, fishermen, prostitutes, slaves and those rejected by the centres of power. If Mark's Gospel was written within a Roman context, the

Christian community of Mark and Peter were those being persecuted by the Roman emperors and were not important within the centrality of empire, citizenship and the city of Rome. Issues of history are interrelated with those of social memory, collective memories and passages within Mark that reflect a social memory that extrapolated what was important rather than what was factual.[90] Such a process, labelled by Michel Foucault as an 'epistemological mutation of history', does not deny the factuality of history but provides for the inclusion of interpretative social processes in which social agency and the role of the writer, translator and victim could be complementary and/or contradictory.[91]

This is where mimesis as a human attribute becomes central to the issue of a social memory. Mimesis as an act of copying and of imitation becomes part of the transmission of social memories not because it allows memories to become tradition, otherwise the act of mimicry should be linked to history (and social historiography), but because it does not. Mimesis is directly linked to a social memory because it takes the form of social creativity, both now and in the future, that does not correspond to a 'collective memory' but is very similar to a genie let out of a bottle, possessing authority and full of creative diversity and magic. In Taussig's understanding, 'the wonder of mimesis lies in the copy drawing on the character and power of the original, to the point whereby the representation may assume that character and that power'.[92]

In a materialistic reading of Mark, the condemnation of Jesus is the result of a clear dismissal of state and state religion by an itinerant preacher and he is condemned by both rather than by one (Mk 15.1–15). His immersion in the society of his time is remembered as outside the realms of religion and politics but without the avoidance of a public conversation with both powers. It is revolutionary in the sense that the teaching provides a third option for a way of life but it is not revolutionary in the political sense, in that Jesus is not looking for the political downfall of Rome so as to assume power himself. Within that materialistic reading of Mark's Gospel, the crucifixion and the lack of an account of the Resurrection in the shorter ending of the text (Mk 15.23–7, 16.3–5) are entirely consistent with a mimesis that does not argue for a deification of personhood and the possibility of cosmic visions of overarching centrality such as those of theologies that dwell on the Atonement, the happy-clappy resurrection and glossolalia or the possibility of an all-reconciling mimetic condition within society arising out of a personal reconciliation with the Christ of faith.

Within a materialistic reading of Mark's empty tomb the body is missing, matter has been moved and the empty tomb shows emptiness to be filled by political intrigue on the one hand and by the development of the materiality of a group of followers and their mimetic memories rather than by a high theology of spiritual understanding of processes that are beyond human understanding and sociopolitical praxis. The longer ending of Mark's Gospel describes Jesus being 'taken up to heaven . . . while they, going out, preached everywhere, the Lord working with them and confirming the word by the signs that accompanied it' (Mk 16.19–20). The signs that accompanied the disciples' return to Galilee in order to recreate their experience somewhere else were the cure of the sick, the inclusion of sinners and the unclean, the possibility that slaves were not part of the values of the Kingdom of God and the life of a community that looked after the widows and orphans and took part in the local life of social communities. I return to the insightful analyses by Marcus Berg:

> Within that framework, the Kingdom of God symbolized the experience of God, an experience known by Jesus himself. The Kingdom of God as the experience of God accounts for Jesus' teaching concerning the way of transformation and the course for Israel. Out of that experience flowed an awareness of a way other than the normative ways of the other renewal movements, one open to the outcasts and not dependent on holiness, but on self-emptying and dying to self and world.[93]

The mimetic condition of a hermeneutical reading of Mark's

Gospel connects directly with the interpretation of the biblical text in order to guide the social life of Christians, located by choice or by fate in the periphery, Christians who take hope and example from Jesus the Galilean and his group of followers, who instead of closing systems of theologizing read the biblical text in order to aid their contextual theologizing within systems of peripheral understanding and the view from the underside of history where Jesus lived and preached the gospel of the Kingdom, not the gospel of power and Christendom, the gospel of prosperity or the gospel of avoidance of the sociopolitical issues of his time.

The hermeneutical model of Mark's Gospel as a tool to read history, past and present, becomes not the traditional Galilee > Jerusalem > ends of the world but Galilee > Jerusalem > mimetic Galilee of the Gentiles or periphery > centre > periphery. This is not a fixed spatial category but an ongoing dialectical category of social interpretation that requires a time-contextual synchronic and diachronic position, subject to modelling peripheries vis-à-vis the biblical text, a subject explored in the following chapter.

3

Centre–Periphery Models

The reading of the Bible by the Christian communities of Latin America created a sense of newness because as a result of their social background members of the communities didn't just follow traditional hermeneutics but they produced hermeneutical transgressions. The clearest text of transgressive revolutionary identity was transcribed by Ernesto Cardenal, and contained within several volumes the conversations that took place within the community of Solentiname in the 1970s and before the Nicaraguan Army destroyed the place.[94] In Solentiname as in many other places the Bible became a tool for Christian action and for community life rather than a text to be analysed by experts. Within those moments of exegetical life in the community the periphery, an isolated and insignificant place in Nicaragua, became the centre of God's voice, God's love and God's salvation.

If in the previous chapters I have explored some social realities within Latin American peripheries and the centrality of Galilee within Jesus' ministry, in this chapter I want to outline the importance of a theologizing that clearly states where the centre and the peripheries are and, as a result, locates the axiom Galilee > Jerusalem > mimetic Galilee of the Gentiles or periphery > centre > periphery within a particular context, in this case the context of the churches in Latin America. The location and understanding of a transgressive hermeneutics of space suggests that the periphery challenges the centre because for the transgressive theologian of the periphery God speaks within the margins of life and society and walks with the poor and the marginalized. In this peripheral location, 'the hermeneutical circle attempts to relate the critical reading of historical reality (with its political, economic, cultural, gender, ethnic, and other oppressions) to a reinterpretation of sacred texts to discern the liberating message of a religious tradition'.[95] That fresh interpretation of the text is made within a *caminhada*, as the Brazilians name the pilgrimage with others and God in the community. As a result, it is difficult to frame a canonical reading of the biblical text or a theologizing that responds to philosophical paradigms rather than the ongoing experience of God within a community.[96]

The use of the social sciences allows the Latin American communities to explore social processes of oppression, liberation and structural sin by reflecting on their daily encounter with others within the periphery and with the help of the biblical text.[97] Through social analysis and the reading of the biblical text they become agents of social reality, even within their condition of marginalization from the State and irreverent globalized unwantedness.[98] Jung Mo Sung has labelled the foundational experience of liberation theology as 'the experience of ethical indignation' and he has clearly spelled out a social example of a marginalized and an unwanted person in society, in case the terms poor or marginalized still remain an intellectual construction and absorption within European theology:

> [I]f we find an individual who is a poor, black, lesbian, AIDS-infected, disabled, ugly, and old prostitute, and still see this individual as a human being in her fundamental dignity, we will be undergoing a spiritual experience of grace (recognition of pure gratuity, beyond all our social conventions) and faith (seeing what is invisible to the eyes of the world).[99]

The concept of centre–periphery, both spatial and cultural, allows us to enter into that social world that is not part of our social conventions by locating ourselves within a social world of discarded individuals of which we would not wish to be part in the first place, but individuals whom we recognize as human beings, loved by God, within the peripheries of society.[100] Those worlds at the margins do not end and they do not cease to exist because of historical changes within the nation state but continue to experience great suffering and cultural creativity.[101]

The concept centre–periphery became very popular in the 1970s in fields as varied as geography, political theory and historical sociology and made its way into Latin American theology through the historic-philosophical contribution of the Argentinean Enrique Dussel.[102] If Dussel allowed the colonial and post-colonial discourse on modernity to be assessed and challenged, my intention in this chapter is to explore (1) centre–periphery within theology and theological method, (2) centre–periphery within society and the individual, and (3) centre–periphery within the spatial contour of the social periphery itself.

Theological Centre–Peripheries

From the beginning of Latin American theology, that is, after the conference of Medellín in 1968, the first generation of theologians found it difficult to dialogue with their European and North American counterparts. There were positions of power about theology, the churches and God. The model centre–periphery was a post-colonial model or a neocolonial model in which theologians of Europe remained at the centre and judged what could be done or what could not be done in other areas of the world. The first generation of Latin American theologians worked within a post-Vatican II mandate and within the established canons of theology. It was only after the ongoing work of the Christian Communities in Brazil, and the theological synthesis of Leonardo Boff, that a new way of perceiving the centre–periphery started to emerge. The process of secularization in the Europe of the late twentieth century meant that the freshness and growing number of Christians in Latin America could not be ignored even when they still remained within the periphery of academic theology. That was not the case within missiology, ecclesiology and the interaction between theology and the social sciences.

Thus, in his analysis of the development of the Ecumenical Association of Third World Theologians (EATWOT) from 1974 to 1983 Dussel recognized that a theology from the periphery had not been accepted by the theological centres in Europe and North America, but at the same time he argued that the emerging Third World theologies, including Latin American theologies, could not be theologies of the centre. Dussel expressed his assessment in a holistic way:

The elaborate theologies of Europe or North America can ignore this new theology or declare that it is unscientific. But just as history gave us the 'modernist crisis' and since then nobody can help thinking historically, so liberation theology present us with objective conditions and in future nobody will be able to avoid thinking in terms of conditioning by class, country, sex, race, etc. This will not just be the one chapter in the history of theology, but it will require a *complete* and *total re-reading of the whole of theology.*[103]

The publication of *Mysterium liberationis* in the early 1990s marked a theological synthesis and the canonical entrance of liberation theology into systematic theology.[104] I am not being absolutely controversial here. Processes of textual acceptance have their own developments and I would rather have a body of writings that can be discussed with other scholars and students. The dynamics referred to by Dussel in 1984 had changed, however, and the new millennium brought the need to rethink theological centres and peripheries once again. Theological methodologies remained divided between those who understood theology as an academic subject (for example, Juan Luis Segundo) and those who remained certain that the process of theologizing was centred within ordinary people, without theological training, of the Christian communities (for example, Leonardo Boff and Gustavo Gutiérrez). Within those two camps it is possible to argue that those who had arrived at the centre were those who considered theology as an academic discipline and those who remained within the periphery were those who considered theologizing as a human act of praxis and reflection within the periphery that surrounds the centre.

I have highlighted Juan Luis Segundo's great contribution to Latin American theology in the previous volume and I would like to leave him behind for a moment and, instead, argue that within the twenty-first century the centre–periphery remains a metaphor for theologizing about the sociopolitical, about oppression and unjust structures from the point of view solely of the periphery. If Latin American theologians managed to re-engage with the history of people and with the history of God, the process of theologizing requires today that theologians analyse social realities in the present rather than in the past. Therefore, my first comment is that theologizing is a synchronic process and that when it becomes diachronic it resembles an academic subject rather than a process of liberation from oppression and of God's act of liberation. It is the 'genitive theologies', understood by Clodovis Boff as political theologies of the European State, that articulated hegemonic theologies of power and control in which the possible fragmentation of theology became articulated through the State, the European Union and the Church as universal encounter for a civilized reconstitution of ecclesiastical and secular power.[105]

The theological methodology of the periphery in daily life is the day to day encounter with realities that cannot be controlled, realities such as sickness, when people are without the means to summon a competent medical doctor, pay hospital bills or buy antibiotics. Marcella Althaus-Reid returns to the core of the theologizing within the periphery when she addresses the return to 'politics and *lo cotidiano* (everyday life)' in order to challenge the fashionable theologizing of genitive theologies 'because class interests, as with racial, cultural, gender and sexual interests, are not profane interests or perspectives irrelevant to theology'.[106] Indeed, incarnational principles and issues of social justice are still of the essence within a theologizing at the periphery. The 'option for the poor' is not an option for a theologizing on issues of poverty, even when such theologizing would have a purpose for Christian activists and other human beings. It is a building-up of respect for the voice of the poor in their everyday lives, their opinions and their assessments of social realities – justice, human dignity and solidarity with other people who are marginalized so that 'if the theology from the poor is to succeed, a clear well-defined poor, as agent of change, needs to be identified in theological discourse'.[107]

It is here that the social sciences become central for the periphery, for the agents within the periphery and for the whole process of theologizing. A theologian within this social milieu could fall under many categories: a resident of the periphery, or/and member of a Christian community, or/and a marginalized social outcast, or a minister of religion within the periphery, or a Christian who is involved in a social organization, a political party, a medical centre, a feeding centre, a drug rehabilitation centre or a resident of a street, neighbourhood or barrio. On a day-to-day basis the theological question that creates oral and written narratives about God is: what is God saying to us today in the context of our social reality, in the context of our community and the gospel of Jesus Christ? The theological narratives arising out of a community discussion or a Bible study group might be very different but they would be the theologies of the poor and the marginalized, they would be the narratives of those who can challenge a centre that would rather have a complete separation between Christian churches and political states, a centre that in a few cases looks after those marginalized within society. Is this kind of theologizing from the periphery serious? Yes, because it addresses the theological narratives of a conversation between a living community and a living God. Would those narratives be objective? No, because they would express the response of a community to the God of Life in a particular context.

It is at this point that historical theology, Christian tradition, and Christian hermeneutics need to be separated. *History* is a narrative about a past event that can be interpreted in many different ways via commonly accepted historical facts. For example, we can all agree that a second council at the Vatican took place from 1962 to 1965 but there are thousands of writings about the history, understanding and impact of Vatican II that express the opinions and stands, sometimes within 'genitive theologies' by theologians and historians alike. A *historical theology* of Vatican II connects the history of the council with the different theologies that were discussed and shows the diversity of those theological positions and the impact they had on the Catholic Church at large. If the documents of Vatican II became part of the *Christian tradition* the ways of implementing the council's resolutions, for example, the change in the positioning of the priest vis-à-vis the altar during the celebration of the Eucharist, only applies to Catholic communities and those who are members of that Christian tradition. The hermeneutics of a social reality that take place within a Christian community in the present are different from historical theology, while in the case of some communities their discussions would be influenced by a particular historical theology or their place in the Christian tradition. However, the point I am making here is that the hermeneutics of everyday life does not include or exclude those who have academic training in historical or systematic theology and those who haven't gone through any of that training. I fully agree with Uriel Molina Oliú, who from his experience of the Christian communities in Nicaragua argued that:

> Anyone who has practical experience of a basic community recognises immediately that the poor have a sort of sixth sense which enables them to grasp the message of the Bible. The poor know that the Bible speaks for them, so that, when they read a passage carefully, they immediately begin to give a very colourful and eloquent expression of it.[108]

Theologizing within the periphery requires that agency is recognized outside the canonical and theological normative organizations, including the churches, but without antagonizing the possibility of the and/both within several fragmented but interrelated layers of the social, the ecclesial and the divine. It requires the acceptance that the victims have become the agents of society's destiny and that a peaceful societal future rests within the possibility of social and divine justice that ultimately brings peace in the 'now' and the 'not yet' of the Kingdom.

Society–Individual

One of the unsolved propositions of theologies from the periphery, liberation theologies and Third World theologies of all kinds has been the role of society and the individual within the process of theologizing and within the salvific action of the God of Life. In my opinion that tension cannot be solved or avoided but needs to be recognized: indeed the fact that there is a tension can have a positive effect and indeed a creative aesthetic tension can have a salvific effect within liberating processes of theologizing.

The tension, also present within European society, arises out of the possibility, and only the possibility, that the individual who believes in God or can recite the Nicene Creed needs to be part of a community. In the grotesque terms of social analysis it has been argued inconsistently that European and North American societies further the cause of the individual while non-Western or Third World societies function within the social structures of a community. While this is a basic truth it is clear that within Latin American theologies there is no work related to a 'theology of self' as individual and there are hundreds if not thousands of theological works that address the people, the poor, the community and the marginalized as large groups with sociological significance or insignificance within the Latin American nation state. That discussion on the individual versus society, in terms of a religious person vis-à-vis a religious community, has been at the forefront of the possibility that an individual may acknowledge Christ as Lord and Saviour without taking any further part in initiation rites or community life. It is remarkable that in the case of Islam this tension is successfully mediated by the fact that a person becomes a Muslim by an individual profession of faith; however, by following the obligation to pray five times a day with others individuals remain part of a mosque, a Muslim community and an extended Muslim family.

Nevertheless, to speak of community has remained a popular and effective way of understanding identity, personal and social, and processes of belonging, of personal adherence to social groups with or without influence within the nation state and within a globalized humanity in which adherence to a religious community does not respect or does not adhere to ideas of localized borders of inclusion/exclusion. Within those complexities of social interaction and according to Vered Amit:

> Community arises out of an interaction between the imagination of solidarity and its realization through social relations and is invested both with powerful effect as well as contingency, and therefore with both consciousness and choice.[109]

In assessing the possibilities and impossibilities of the individual–society axis I would argue that a dividing cultural and socioreligious crisis has taken place. The cultural crisis has taken place with the rise of individualism, secularization and consumerism among those who have prospered since the return of democratic regimes and the signing of free trade agreements with China and other Asian countries. Further, the alliance of the military regimes with the United States had already started a cultural crisis of change in history whereby Latin America was closer to the values and markets of Europe in the 1960s and somehow less open to a close cooperation with the United States. Today, the values of marketing opportunities and the life of free choice as lived in the United States seem to be the overwhelming arching parameters of social mimesis and social aspiration for those who can afford that kind of life. The cultural hegemony of the television and the media have managed to convince the majority of Latin American public opinion that such a style of life is desirable. This may be seen in Chile, for example, where obesity levels continue to increase, a trend encouraged by the popularity of fast food among office workers looking for an affordable lunch.

The rise of Pentecostalism and Evangelicalism within Latin America has remained steady and one of the social forces among the poor and the marginalized.[110] Among those forces, Christian groups that stress the individual choice of acknowledging Christ as Lord in a personal and emotional manner rather than baptism as a community ritual of admission into a symbolic/ritual community of believers provide a quick entry into a world that promises lots to the poor but alienates them from movements for social justice, workers' rights or local possession of lands taken by foreign corporations. The problem becomes ever larger and more pronounced by the fact that individual choices of a personalized Christianity reflect a choice for a gospel of prosperity rather than an option for the poor and the marginalized. While I do not doubt here the honesty of Christian groups that proclaim individualism in belief within Latin America, I am arguing that Latin American theologians in general have used the sociology of religion in which groups and communities accept, reject and produce theological narratives about God and the God of Life in Latin America, which thus become part of the social fabric of the marginalized rather than just a consolation in times of trouble and affliction.

As a result of these changes, cultural, sociopolitical and religious, it is more difficult to articulate the common trends in religious practice and sociopolitical developments related to religion in the future. The different socioreligious components operate at different levels of consciousness and provide religious responses to different phenomena. Within that diversity of religious practice or the absence of it Brazil remains an example of a country where diversity in religious practice, including African religions, coexist and are at the heart of the lives of the majority of the poor and marginalized of the urban areas and the rural periphery. Within a country with a Catholic majority the diversity in religious practice remains a possibility for both individuals and communities, creating a mimetic sociability of non-exclusion or exclusivity and, as stated by Pope Benedict XVI in his 2007 visit to Brazil, making 'the promotion of the human person the axis of solidarity, especially towards the poor and abandoned'.[111]

If one is to investigate the centre–periphery further, more research must be done by recording individual voices from the periphery, because those voices bring out social and theological narratives from the periphery into the centre.[112] After all, periphery and centre, society and individual are directly connected with one another to the point where, if the individual within the periphery is going to acquire some hope, it would be because groups within the periphery manage to negotiate spaces and human dignity with those who control them, located for the most part within the centre. Individuals and groups assume a particular agency and develop a certain manner of theologizing vis-à-vis their location within the 'now' and 'not yet' of the Kingdom of God. If the personal preoccupation of a person is with attaining an assurance of salvation that person would most probably behave as an individual and make a distinction between religion as a vehicle for personal salvation and the social realities that exist within the nation state. If a person is concerned about religion and its practice within a community in order to attain salvation then most probably that person would engage with social realities knowing that the role of the community within the nation state is extremely important.

A critique of Latin American theology has been that it has worked with analytical categories that are not fluid enough and, as a result, has opted for the poor, an option that has no bearing, theologically speaking, within the context. Those criticisms have missed the fact that 'the poor' as a sociological category can be interpreted in a particular social context as a prisoner without a name or a poor person called Juanita. The same criticism could be applied to the analytical terminology of Vatican II when the council mentions 'the people of God', after all an ambiguous term with several possible interpretations. However, the same discussion on 'the poor and the marginalized' could lead to a further understanding on the social and ecclesial limitations that are faced by individuals in Latin America, a fact that could explain why Latin American theologians are not writing about human fulfilment and the personal choices in personal fulfilment or the use of personal talents for personal means and ends. Another criticism outlined by José Comblin has been of the possibility of introducing politics into Christian ritual, thus bringing processes of social conscientization into the liturgy, a process that alienated many people who wanted a clear distinction between a moment of worship and a moment of social action. Comblin argues that:

> Religious and liturgical acts are of a specific nature and should be respected. Worship cannot be turned into a means for something else, like political consciousness-raising. That is how many people were alienated from liberation movements. An attempt was made to force the movements on people at the wrong time.[113]

The rise of spiritualism and individual spiritual experiences suggests that there is still a search for a spiritual connection with a world different from that of the market, within a search for individual fulfilment and the self-expression of the individual in community. The individual remains created by God, creative, intelligent and capable of a loving response towards God and towards others but, in order to exist socially, requires not only to be part of a social, political or sociostructural group but needs to develop individual talents and individual responses to God and the community. An individual must belong to a community in order to grow in personal faith, a faith tailored by the experience of a community but shaped according to different spiritualities, personal experiences and the life journey. The Latin American self exists as a distinct cultural self as far as the individual is shaped and influenced by a Latin American context, and a person remains open to the social and the social realities of the poor and the marginalized as far as that person remains affected and influenced by the realities of the poor and the marginalized.

A criticism of the 1970s' overexaggeration of society and community has been the possibility that the individual was denied existence by religious and political movements whose stress was on 'the people' (*el pueblo*) or the State (*la gente, el país*). However, the values behind that overuse of community allowed the poor to have the opportunity to explore their lives and to take part in the exploration of the individual through the arts, through music, poetry, painting and dance. Recent theological critiques of the theologizing of the masses within the churches have pointed precisely to the possibility that an individual might be gay or lesbian and therefore a different kind of individual operating within a theological anthropology which is too narrow for anthropological developments of the self within Latin America.[114]

Nevertheless, the traditional view and mostly applicable to Latin American society via a process of theologizing has been summarized by José Ignacio González when he wrote in the canonical work for liberation theology *Mysterium liberationis*:

> I am not trying to appraise this difference, but I do consider it a *symptomatic fact*. The West continues to be the heir (and at times the slave) of the individualism of Modernism, characterized by the 'discovery of the subject', as it has been said repeatedly. The novelty of Latin American theology is the extent to which the faith experience and the spiritual personal experience are communitarian experiences in the way they are carried out, but often in their context as well.[115]

It is the supra-individual, above society's needs and above individual's wants who was in the past able to develop talents associated with the aristocracies and the well-to-do. The rest, and the majority, were struggling to find bread for their families with no time for other tasks within urban centres in which the sense of patronage and social relations still requires people who need something to spend a considerable time on the road in order to request help for goods or services that in Europe and North America are taken for granted. For example, my family used to have home help from teenagers from the South of Chile, who couldn't go to secondary school (there were none in the area), and who were known to a family that had a debt of gratitude towards my family. M had had an accident while farming in the Puerto Montt area and his arm had been badly damaged by a harvester machine. After being transferred to a Santiago public hospital he needed ongoing physiotherapy and several operations in order to regain the use of the arm. He remained at my mother's home, in and out of hospital for a period of a year. His wife was a teacher in a local primary school, and was able to recommend a girl aged 16+ who could come and help my mother at home in Santiago, who would live with us and attend school in the evening. Most of those girls would find a partner and eventually settle in Santiago and have several children in the poorest areas of Santiago, areas without an electricity meter and unpaved roads. Whenever there was a need, for example, a sick child needing some medicine, the girl would call my mother from a public phone, already located a couple of kilometres away, and would have to take three buses to get to my mother's place where my mother would give her the money to buy medicines plus money for the bus fares. Years later, when I visited her and her family, it took me three hours to get there and I met a courageous woman who had previously taken care of me and my brothers living in a shack without water, toilets or electricity, still very grateful that I had gone to drink tea with them, with tea and sugar that I had brought because they didn't have anything and were living on beans prepared by a communal group of women aided by the local Catholic parish. Those women secured a safe passage to other shacks and other inhumane places of human habitation and were extremely generous with the dispossessed and the persecuted.

How can we stress the individual in those circumstances? Is our theological anthropology adequate to understand any theologizing about it? I must be honest here; my personal response when I was a university student was to move to a poor area in order to share that kind of life so as to deal with my personal guilt and slowly to be educated into a different kind of life and a different kind of community values where God was not a comforter but a friend and a defender. Years later, and in another unexpected return to Chile, I was at my mother's place one Sunday afternoon when one of her daughters arrived with a bag of oysters for me that had been transported all the way by bus from Southern Chile (12 hours by bus) and another couple of hours through Santiago in order to welcome my safe return and in gratitude for being part of those who stood with them when gas canisters and security forces arrived. In theologizing and when theologians make too much of the self and the creative individual I think of them, with scepticism, gratitude and anger.

The primacy of the individual vis-à-vis the community was stressed by Pope Benedict XVI in his 2007 visit to Brazil and he was clearly direct when addressing the Brazilian bishops on matters of truth, obedience and teaching.[116] He didn't mention Latin American theology in particular during that speech but he certainly stressed individual sin (rather than structural sin), personal and individual confession (rather than communal absolution), an individual response to Jesus Christ, an individual participation in the Eucharist (rather than a communal theological celebration of life), and he finally urged the Brazilian bishops to be responsible catechists, teachers and evangelizers by remembering that they were individually responsible for the role of teaching and of catechesis.[117] This last point was most probably a clear shift from the stress on communities and their catechists fully in charge of encouraging and teaching the Brazilian faithful. The 'popular church' and the emergence of the Brazilian base communities was being clearly replaced by the church's *magisterium* centred on Christ and truth rather than on any other social response to experience and sociability.

Despite those shifts towards the individual, a very European and Roman approach, the communities in Brazil and elsewhere have shown that Christianity is a communal celebration. The threat of Pentecostalism can be interpreted as a theological acceptance of a personal call to live by the Bible but also can be interpreted as providing a celebratory context of spontaneity and emotional outbursts more akin to the Latin American self, particularly in Brazil, than to the Germanic approach to perfection and precision within the celebration of the liturgy, another detail mentioned by Benedict XVI.

Without considering social realities, it is almost impossible to discuss individual and community because the completely free and autonomous individual does not exist. A person lives within a particular social reality and while an increasing number of European and North Americans can enhance their individuality through education, arts or even ways of dressing that is not the reality for most Latin Americans. Economic conditions of inequality prevent the majority from even thinking about themselves because the primary daily task is to try to acquire the basic human needs, taken for granted by those who are looked after by the State in Europe or North America.

Challenging Agencies

Within a Latin American theologizing, agency becomes a challenging point of discussion because the one who has agency can constrain other non-canonical or non-acceptable theologies or can ignore or suppress other peripheries and other social realities. With that object in mind within the periphery, the centre has a role to further understanding of the possibility of diversity in the whole of social life, religious or non-religious. The job of the theologian at the periphery is to facilitate the possibility of interaction between believers and non-believers and their communities and to ensure that all rights of conscience are respected. Within that difficult relation of centre–periphery diversity society can create relativism by suggesting that it is not by knowing and experiencing a particular tradition that people can engage in a meaningful dialogue with others. In practice, diverse traditions work very well together within the periphery; thus, the danger and the only possible danger are not the diversity of the periphery but the fundamentalism of the centre.

One contemporary example of these difficulties between centre and periphery has been the attempt by the Vatican to change the agency of the Basic Christian Communities for the Church Movements as agents of evangelization within the Church and as agents of dialogue outside Christian enclaves. The problem with this ongoing ecclesiastical approach has become clearer: if the Basic Christian Communities were willing to engage with cooperative community projects with others, civil society and other faiths, the Church movements are inward looking and do not pretend to be there to work together with movements outside the Catholic Church. Catherine Pepinster, editor of *The Tablet* commented on that situation in the following words:

> This is another example of a basic structural problem in the modern Catholic Church: ideas and insights flow downwards from the top easily enough, but move hardly at all in an upwards direction. The result is a longer and longer list of issues where the periphery has difficulty with what the centre is saying. Eventually the two perceptions of what needs to be done have little in common: the leaders have become unharnessed from the led.[118]

For the outsider, that is someone who is not fully committed to the Catholic Church or to any particular church, there is a historical complexity within the ecclesiastical structures that is completely overwhelming. It is no surprise that the Brazilian Bishops printed a shorter kind of Catholic catechism with the name *I am Catholic, I Live My Faith*, a 151-page booklet with the essentials of the Catholic faith, to coincide with Benedict XVI's arrival in Brazil.[119] The power of persuasion of the Pentecostals in Brazil does not come from bureaucratic agencies but from the street-to-street dissemination of single pages with biblical passages and invitations to worship God in community.

Already Leonardo Boff got in deep doctrinal troubles with his theological investigation into the early Christian communities and the power that they had because of their simplicity. The periphery of slaves worshipping in Rome and listening to the stories about Jesus of Nazareth had the power to challenge

Vatican structures in the twentieth century. It is possible to argue once again that, despite Benedict XVI's emphasis on obedience and truth with Christ as its centre, the power of Christian love could make all the difference. However, the Church as teacher, the preferred model of the former Cardinal Ratzinger, needs to disappear in order to serve others, be they Christians or not. It is a servant Church that would make the difference within the Latin American periphery where theological narratives of deep intellectual resonances are not really a daily occurrence but where thousands of Christians theologize by asking questions about the role of the Church, the presence of God and the realities to come in the afterlife, a natural human preoccupation that competes side by side with questions about the presence of God in the contemporary world and among the poor and the marginalized of the periphery.

Is it possible to trust that God's agency has been given to those with open hearts at the periphery of society? Is it possible to find joy in the fact that God has empowered through baptism all Christians and all those who seek the presence of God? Is it possible to serve the poor and the marginalized within the periphery without finding theology, and Latin American theology, disturbing? My initial proposition is that it is possible and even desirable. Thus, in the following chapter I explore the nature and role of a servant Church located fully at the periphery where theologizing becomes a daily activity and not only the academic and intellectual activity of learned theologians, teachers of truth and keepers of the Christian tradition.

Part 2

Contemporary Challenges

4

A Servant Church of the Periphery

In the previous chapter I located the Church as community within the periphery and in relation to social phenomena as well as political events. The role of the Church within a development from apologetics to service is of a community that in celebrating faith, hope and resurrection becomes one with the victims of oppression and poverty. Further, in assuming the victims within the periphery are those closer to the values of the Kingdom the Church needs to learn and shape her own community life by learning from the periphery and the God of Life who lives at the periphery – the centre of value-added Kingdom of God.

In this chapter I explore further the role of a servant Church that exists to serve rather than to be served and that aids the coming of the Kingdom by following her master in his attitudes of fellowship with sinners and of service to the neediest within society.

A Diversity of Models

Over the years and particularly after Vatican II there have been many theological evaluations of the image that portrays the Church vis-à-vis the contemporary world. Indeed, over the centuries since her beginnings the Church has changed circumstances, history and location vis-à-vis the world and the poor and the marginalized. The single monolithic model of one Church does not exist because theological reflections vary and because councils and popes have overemphasized one model rather than another.

The use of models for comparative ecclesiology, as outlined by Avery Dulles SJ, could be useful to think if not to dream of the Church as a non-monolithic institution. These models are described by theologies of liberation; it can be a community that changes according to needs and certainly can serve the poor and the marginalized by reflecting on itself as well as on the contemporary realities. Dulles argued that:

> The peculiarity of models, as contrasted with aspects, is that we cannot integrate them into a single synthetic vision on the level of articulate, categorical thought. In order to do justice to the various aspects of the Church, as a complex reality, we must work simultaneously with different models. By a kind of mental juggling act, we have to keep several models in the air at once.[120]

Models allow us to compare through a taxonomy that perceives differences and theological mutual ties, be they models of text or of the Church. For Dulles, the use of models becomes fruitful when they are used in the comparative as 'no good ecclesiology is exclusively committed to a single model of the Church'.[121] Dulles is correct in that the comparative method allows the extrapolation of a variety of ecclesial situations and if I were to choose two models I would certainly choose the sacramental model together with the servant model. However, I would also suggest that the models of the Church refer ultimately to a model of God because it is the Church as missionary extension of Christ that concerns us here, a concern with a Church that expressed the preoccupation by God with the poor and the marginalized and a mission of the Church that models herself on Christ the servant of lepers, prostitutes and all those afflicted. Thus, according to Vatican II:

> Since this mission continues and, in the course of history, unfolds the mission of Christ, who was sent to evangelize the poor, then the Church, urged on by the Spirit of Christ, must walk the road Christ himself walked, a way of poverty and

86

obedience, of service and self-sacrifice even to death, a death from which he emerged victorious by his resurrection.[122]

A model of the servant historical Jesus goes hand in hand with the model of a servant Church that arises out of the Christ of faith within the possibility and impossibility of a theology that continues to be defined as *fides quaerens intellectum*.[123] If a comparative model of God, together with that of servant is required, Sallie McFague has intimated a challenging metaphor in 'God as lover of the world', as the one who remains in love with the sinner within a reality in which 'sin is the turning-away not from a transcendental power but from interdependence with all other human beings, including the matrix of being from whom all life comes'.[124]

The model of a servant Church was the model highlighted by the Second Vatican Council, a model that responded to a call for *aggiornamento* and for a Church of the poor supported first by John XXIII and later by Paul VI. Thus, the beautiful opening of the 'Pastoral Constitution on the Church in the Modern World' (7 December 1965) proclaimed that:

> The joy and hope, the grief and anguish of the men of our time, especially of those who are poor or afflicted in any way, are the joy and hope, the grief and anguish of the followers of Christ as well. Nothing that is genuinely human fails to find an echo in their hearts.[125]

Within that understanding Vatican II also elaborated the concept of 'the people of God', those who, having been touched by God, remain at his service within a Church in which different ministries and calls are exercised and in which all have a 'supernatural appreciation of the faith (*sensus fidei*) of the whole people, when, "from the bishops to the least of the faithful" they manifest a universal consent in matters of faith and morals'.[126] Further, 'the holy People of God shares also in Christ's prophetic office' throughout the many different nations of the world where the Church is present, so that *qui Romae*

sedet, Indos scit membrum suum esse.[127] Within that presence
of the Church among the different nations of the worlds there
are those who are not Christians and therefore Vatican II stated
that 'those who, through no fault of their own, do not know the
Gospel of Christ or his Church, but who nevertheless seek God
with a sincere heart, and, moved by grace, try in their actions to
do his will as they know it through the dictates of their conscience – those too may achieve eternal salvation'.[128] Within
those who are closer to the Church are Muslims because they
'hold the faith of Abraham, and together with us they adore the
one, merciful God, mankind's judge of the last day'.[129]

It is that mandate of common understanding with other
faiths and with an understanding about the agency of salvation
in God's hands that triggered the Latin American bishops
gathered in Medellín in 1968 to respond with a pastoral plan of
engagement with Latin American society. The prophetic role of
announcing the Kingdom of God was taken very seriously, in
the knowledge that any prophetic office required an understanding of the social and the provision of food and aid to the
poor and the needy.[130] The Latin American *aggiornamento*
went further and the service of Christian charity became questioned by a reflection on the prophetic and Christian prophetic
attitudes of Christians, including theologians, within Latin
American society.

The New Brazilian Model

If I return to these discussions that were already part of the
1970s and 1980s it is because Benedict XVI in his 2007 visit to
Brazil and addressing those taking part in the opening Eucharist
of the Fifth General Meeting of Latin American bishops at the
shrine of Aparecida, Brazil, emphasized two different models:
the missionary model and the teaching model.[131] If theological
discussions on models were just academic discussions this
would not matter; however, the address by Benedict XVI has an
ongoing impact on pastoral plans implemented by traditional

bishops appointed by his predecessor John Paul II and who, in the majority, prefer models *ad intra*, pastoral and spiritual models heavily bounded by doctrine and by apologetics, rather than by prophetic statements of service outside the Christian community. The fact that the majority of Christians and the majority of theologians at the centre and the periphery of Latin America are Catholics makes this discussion ever more central to the theologies of the periphery or the possible absence of them in the twenty-first century.

The missionary model outlined by Benedict XVI is heavily Christ-centric and heavily apologetic because it plans to encounter two different social realities: the lack of understanding of the faith by most Catholics in Latin America and the desertions that followed as a result of the preaching by other Christian groups, particularly Pentecostals and groups described by the Latin American bishops as 'pseudo-spiritual'.[132] The theological movement is from within the Church to others with a pedagogical dialectic of doctrinal defence and communal reaffirmation. This is the model that was adopted by the Catholic Church in Argentina under the military junta, a separation of the doctrinal and the spiritual from the sociopolitical, sinful and unjust within Latin American society. The model comes from the centre and remains at the centre while the periphery is welcomed to take part in the possibility of accepting and celebrating the eternal truths of which the Church is custodian. The signs of a diverse Christianity and an inculturated liturgical celebration start to disappear, so that Rome becomes the absolute centre and local manifestations of music and art are still superseded by the European organ and the European orchestras, as was made clear during the visit of Benedict XVI to Brazil. In his address to the Brazilian bishops and the celebration of vespers at the São Paulo Cathedral it was clear that the orchestra played music that resembled the processions at the centre of the Roman Empire rather than the celebration of life by a diversified, multicultural and even Afro-American and Amazonian Brazil.

In itself Benedict XVI's model is dependent on that of John

Paul II, with emphasis on catechesis and a deeper understanding of the faith within the Church. It would not be expected otherwise than that a religious community would not try to encourage members to learn about their religious symbols and the credal assertions to which they adhere. Indeed, the model of catechesis through Basic Christian Communities and the daily reading of the Bible was the successful model implemented by the Church in Brazil. The model, though, has one worrying aspect, the centrality of spiritual realities, and one significant omission, the centrality of the Kingdom of God, as outlined in the inaugural address of the meeting of Latin American bishops at Aparecida.

In Benedict XVI's speeches in Brazil there is certainly a centred Church that can teach the faithful: they are to be evangelized and educated rather than 'the people of God' including the pope and the bishops needing to be evangelized and educated further in the faith. Within that slight separation of clergy = church there is a slight rupture from the Vatican II model in which all believers are 'the people of God' and therefore are members of the Church in so far as they have been baptized.[133] Within that model of a teaching Church that holds the truth, Benedict XVI asked questions about reality, material and spiritual realities, and declared the inability of twentieth-century models to deal with reality, that is, Marxism and capitalism. Further, he asserted that 'only those who recognize God recognize reality', an interesting movement away from materialistic philosophies, atheism and agnosticism. Thus, the spiritual realm becomes central to the world and therefore to the encounter of a teaching Church with the realities of the contemporary world. In moving towards a more spiritual sense of primal realities, Benedict XVI contradicts two important trends of the late twentieth century within Catholicism: the development of African theologies with their integration of the corporeal and the world of the spirit, and the dialogue, sometimes very productive, of materialistic theologies and those of an ecological nature centred upon discourses of common materiality and our stewardship of the earth. Those trends of possible dialogue cannot, in my opinion, be set aside but must be considered important for the dialogue and engagement with contemporary globalization.

The Kingdom's Model

The position of Christianity and of Roman Catholic Christianity within Latin America is of a majority that can exercise influence, social and political, because of the numbers of citizens who consider themselves Catholics. However, a theology that exalts the centre and the power of knowledge by the centre can only lead to a social isolation and therefore to the 'love of God' to the detriment of the 'love of neighbour'. It is not a coincidence that Gutiérrez and Sobrino considered that the Kingdom of God was the all-embracing umbrella that could allow the 'love of God' to move side by side with the 'love of neighbour'. Sobrino's sense of an oral theology that predates any written theology is useful here because for him:

> Now, in this world, the utopia hoped for is not any utopia, but the hope that life, as the primal fact of surviving, the dignity of outcasts and basic solidarity – justice, in a word – may be possible. Therefore, without being naïve or anachronistic, there is no doubt that the Third World, much more than others, presents a historical reality somehow analogous to that in which the very notion of a 'Kingdom of God' arose.[134]

The contradiction between models could be solved here by excluding the Kingdom of God as the all-embracing reality, but in the biblical reading it is clear that the eschaton remains 'here and now' but 'not yet'. Thus it cannot be the only reality that unites the Church and society. Since the 1970s, the idea of a utopia was firmly based on a prophetic model of the Church totally involved with the poor and the marginalized, with the difficulties inherent within a prophetic model that, combined with the language of contemplation, starts to bring internal conversion and structural conversion together. Thus, Gutiérrez has argued that:

> Without prophecy, the language of contemplation runs the risk of failing to bite on the history in which God acts and in which we meet him. And without the mystical dimension, prophetic language can narrow its horizons and weaken its perception of the One who makes all things new.[135]

The models of Church certainly match the different responses to minority/majority issues. The majority can teach others because it has the support of a majority of people: thus, it has to make sure that there are mechanisms of inclusiveness that allow the possibility of dialogue and cooperation. The prophetic model tends to appear in the midst of oppression and when large numbers of people question structures, considered by them oppressive and inadequate. That was the case of prophetic pronouncements against poverty and injustice within the nation state by the Church and other political bodies and the prophetic pronouncements by women and other marginalized sectors of the Catholic Church after Vatican II and throughout the development of liberation theologies.

It is my proposition here that the model of a servant Church not only corresponds to the biblical analysis expounded in a previous chapter but also is the model of the Kingdom where, following from Vatican II, 'the search for truth, however, must be carried out in a manner that is appropriate to the dignity of the human person and his or her social nature, namely, by free enquiry with the help of teaching or instruction, communication and dialogue'.[136]

In terms of sociological models of group immersion and group dynamics, the majority dictates what is right; in democratic terms, those who have the majority of votes within a national electorate organize a government. In terms of the Kingdom that social majority are the poor and the marginalized of Latin America and they dictate the agenda. The political model for that religious community, be it the institutional model portrayed by Benedict XVI or the servant model of Pedro Casaldáliga, relates to values that contradict political means and ends but must work within the realities of a world in which God is not absolutely present within political institutions. Avery Dulles reminds us of the difference: 'In the institutional models, the official Church teaches, sanctifies, and rules with the authority of Christ' while in the servant model 'the Church takes the world as a properly theological locus, and seeks to discern the signs of the times' so that 'it seeks to operate on the frontier between the contemporary world and the Christian tradition (including the Bible), rather than simply apply the latter as a measure of the former'.[137]

The attitude of cooperation and service was richly expressed by Vatican II's expectation that 'Christians can yearn for nothing more ardently than to serve the men of this age with an ever growing generosity and success' and 'joining forces with all who love and practice justice'.[138] That ongoing service was channelled through the Basic Christian Communities, localized groups of Christians that functioned within the structure of a parish and a diocese and that in their daily life served the needy and the marginalized of the neighbourhood. The Latin American bishops at Santo Domingo reiterated their centrality warning that, in cases where the ecclesial centrality of those communities is not properly defined, they could be manipulated for political ends, a preoccupation that had become acute over several years because of the appointment of more traditional and power-centred bishops by John Paul II and Benedict XVI.[139]

The tension is between the models of the Church in which the communities are perceived as agents of the private realm and those in which the challenge to a pastoral model becomes centred in critiques *ad extra* rather than *intra*. For example, Iván Petrella criticizes, and rightly so, the spiritualist positions of the radical orthodoxy movement and its disciples, in this case Daniel Bell Jr's position in his *Liberation Theology after the End of History*.[140] Basically, Petrella contests Bell's separation of the role of the Church from civil society and advocates a further economic understanding according to which capitalism and civil society vis-à-vis capitalism become the milieu for a model of the Church which is not dissociated from society's concerns.[141] In a way, both Petrella and Bell provide narratives that have been intellectualized and secularized *ad extra* while the critique still assumes the model of the Church as hierarchical, structural and institutional. The Church is located outside the possibility of a narrative by the poor and marginalized because it is perceived as institutional, grandiose and immanent. I am afraid that it is more likely that Bell and Petrella could discuss this and find some agreement with Benedict XVI because what is missing from their model is the pastoral agency of a Latin American Church that, despite criticisms by John Milbank, Stanley Hauerwas or Daniel Bell, remains in situ, in the context of Latin America, serving the poor and the marginalized despite the debates in North America regarding their authority, credibility or success.[142]

Maybe the Roman/institutional model of Benedict XVI also portrays the experience of a German theologian who has managed to unite a Catholic world by some theological coercion but has understood that the strength of the Latin American Church has come from within itself, and the enemy has been the European model that seems to have accepted the situation whereby it has to live with empty pews and empty seminaries. The unresolved challenges to North American theologies by ethnic minorities have also been challenged by the crisis of child abuse by Catholic clergy, a minority, but a symptom of what conditions of power and centrality can lead to.

The servant model of Church within the periphery is very close to the model of the early Church. Thus it is a very scriptural model, with an eschatological sense of deliverance, hope and solidarity. Within that model God is the primary mover and the preoccupation is not how to perpetuate the institution but how to serve, to love and to share with those rejected by society, including in that action the love of God and the love of neighbour. The possible abstraction of the values of the Kingdom, even regarding justice and peace, disappear when confronted with the realities faced by the scriptural community of the New

Testament so that, for Avery Dulles, 'The New Testament per-
sonalizes the Kingdom. It identifies the Kingdom of God with
the gospel, and both of them with Jesus.'[143]

The Kingdom model still proclaims the possibility of theological and social diversity without relativism; it argues that as
it was in the early Church of Rome Christians lived in the
periphery, slaves and persecuted, being brought together in the
megapolis by the sacramental presence of the breaking of bread.
Indeed, the breaking of bread, either in the form of a daily sharing of a meal or the actual celebration of the Eucharist, brings
people together, as human beings first, then as co-pilgrims of
the Kingdom. I am sure that there is a contemporary need to use
words such as Christian fellowship in order to express the
normal and human experience of eating and drinking together.
This value becomes ever more important within the large urban
centres, within the peripheries of those centres where, as in the
case of the Brazilian megapolis, human beings need, according
to João Batista Libânio, consolation and social support. The
new charismatic and Pentecostal groups provide an immediate
emotional consolation while the social programmes run by the
Catholic Church provide a 'process of consciousness-raising
associated with immediate and charitable help'.[144] Other groups
proclaim other social truths and other models of prosperity and
acceptance.

The process of theologizing by those in the periphery
becomes ever more problematic when it leaves the mirror of the
Kingdom because it is in the exotic peripheries that magicians,
market-traders, healers, preachers, prostitutes, drug dealers
and priests interact with each other. The periphery is not a dull
world but a creative one and a world filled with chaotic noise,
abandonment and drink. Alcoholics and those who are looking
for a moment of sociability end up in bars, occasions that could
end up in violence and in death. If somebody has not experienced the periphery it is very difficult for that person to understand the biblical passages on the Kingdom of God, on talents
and parables to be multiplied, on miracles and supra-natural
phenomena that speak of a God who, powerful on the one

hand, remains a servant waiting for others and giving the agency and the choice to others, on the other. In the interpretation by Ignacio Ellacuría, 'whatever critical reading be made of the miracles, there can be no doubt that the primitive community saw, in the satisfaction of altogether concrete needs, the sign of the presence of the kingdom – to the point where the satisfaction of these necessities on occasion led the multitude to erroneous interpretations of the character of Jesus' prophetism'.[145] The fear of doing the wrong thing or the possibility of erroneous conclusions is what I would describe as the fear of theologizing or the fear involved in the process of theologizing. Let me illustrate this with a personal recollection.

When in 1977 I ventured for the first time into a large urban area of Santiago that I still remember as dark, always muddy and with shady characters on the street corners. I felt fear. It was not the fear of the political activist who feared to be caught but the physical fear of walking in places where if I were to be attacked by someone with a knife I would not have had a chance. I noticed that many times people walked with me from an urban shack to the bus stop but inside the bus I also felt fear. I learned to live with fear and the fear didn't go away. It was like a performer who feels the adrenaline pumping before the performance, but the fear I felt was intense because I felt on my own and without agency. Yes, on arrival at the entrance to the shanty town I could choose not to walk further but it was an abandonment of my own choice and will that led me there, in order to share a few thoughts on the biblical text or to try to support a youth outreach towards drug addicts. After a few weeks I felt myself supported by those young people, and the values of solidarity and companionship which I experienced came from the poor not from my own strength. In 1986, as General Pinochet escaped assassination, I was urged by a priest to get into a van because I was on the wrong side of the city, the police were searching and there was no way that friends were to allow further repression. Indeed, I was brought to my mother's flat in the respectable side of the city as the morning news on the following day reported that several men had been shot by the security forces, one for every military escort who was killed in the ambush of Pinochet's entourage. This is what I wouldn't like anybody to experience but these are the experiences that make the theologian realize that the poor and marginalized have an agency and strength for solidarity and for the Kingdom that those of us who were raised in better economic conditions lack.

It is that immersion in the periphery and in history that makes a theologian understand the God of Life as present in the agency of the poor and the marginalized. For 'the God of life is present in human history; this presence reaches its supreme and unsurpassed expression in the incarnation of the Son'.[146] The incarnational principle of servanthood is the example: God sent his Son into human history, and thus all his followers must live there where he was immersed, with the needy, the poor and the lonely. In other words, with the losers of this globalized community, those who do not count within the statistics apart from the fact that they ruin the possible promotions of politicians and technocrats by hindering better statistics on wealth and prosperity.

That experiencing of emptying is the experience of many human beings who, in solidarity with other human beings, enter worlds where they would rather not live and pay a price. It is the case of Norman Kember, for example, a pacifist and Christian activist, who, not happy with his armchair pacifism, decided to join a group of Christian observers and witnesses to dialogue, and in 2005 went to Iraq for a short visit that became a nightmare when he was kidnapped together with three other companions, one of them, Tom Fox, being killed by their captors. Rescued by the coalition armed forces of the West he forgave his captors and declined testifying against them in the Iraqi Courts. Kember's experience is an example of the ongoing reflection and the lessons always learned by those who risk living in the periphery when he writes on his experience of being a hostage in Iraq:

I have always had difficulties with the problem of evil. How can a God of compassion and mercy and love have created men and women so capable of forgetting compassion, mercy and love in their dealings with their fellow human beings? I accept that the Christian experience of a God who suffers with us provides a way into answering the problem . . . This remains an unresolved dilemma and I continue to try to act in the faith that God is compassionate, merciful and loving.[147]

Indeed, this is the dilemma of the one who serves and of the servant Church: how to serve without full understanding? How to break barriers and become incarnated without fear of error? How to embrace a rejected human being without worrying about the consequences? How to love one's enemies without advocating the possibility of harming them? How to be located in the periphery and how to learn from the periphery?

Theologians can lose their souls and their minds by trying to articulate philosophical arguments about a God without a body and a God without a heart; the periphery is the best cure for such a process. Anybody who has helped a charity helping the Third or Fourth Worlds and those who have totally identified themselves with other people, their realities and their needs, have experienced this kenosis, this emptying of oneself in order to fill it with other peoples' realities, words and images. Those of us who have lived away from our places of birth have emptied ourselves many times in order to survive and eventually have come to a process of love in which understanding ceases to exist, ceases to matter and is out of our books because that understanding comes out of the lives of those who serve and those who, like Ignacio Ellacuría, the assassinated Jesuit in El Salvador, ceased to worry about carrying others because at the end others were carrying him, until martyrdom and death.

Theologizing is a process that comes out of a liberating praxis, out of a diverse way of empowering people, and being empowered by the lives of the poor and the marginalized in the periphery. It is only by re-examining those beacons of hope that remain examples of service and kenosis that one can reflect once again on the process of theologizing from the periphery. That process of kenosis experienced by Norman Kember or Ignacio

Ellacuría is the daily ordinary process of those who live and serve others at the periphery, without realizing that their process of theologizing is deep because it reflects the central commandments of loving God and neighbour in their daily lives. The victims, 'the crucified', those mentioned once and again by Jon Sobrino are the servants at the forefront of God's action; we are mere spectators of such realities until we empty ourselves of many idols and many false Gods, until we theologize without understanding and with fear in our lives, fear of not following the values of the Kingdom and the values of a theology that exercises kenosis with a constant fellowship with sinners and those rejected by society.[148]

Our fear of the victims as the fear of others, including fellow Christians, plays a central role against the possibility of serious theologizing within the periphery, seriously understood as playful, community oriented and, in the words of Marcella Althaus-Reid, 'indecent' theologizing.[149] There is no doubt that interfaith dialogue becomes a sign of the Kingdom and that, regardless of the apprehensions that one Christian group could have of another, the poor and marginalized are central to the preoccupation of many Christian groups, many groups within civil society, and those who do not profess any religious symbolic affiliation but remain very human and very spiritual in their lives and actions.

In the following chapter I examine some of the social and theological questions that an interfaith dialogue entails within contemporary Latin America. In asking those questions, I am relocating the interfaith question from within a single majority Church into a large variety of groups that consider themselves Christians, but am reiterating my position that, following the methodology outlined by Latin American theologians, the interfaith dialogue can only be fruitful if the poor and the marginalized of the periphery remain agents of their lives and educate the groups engaged in interfaith dialogue in solidarity with the values of the periphery which are ultimately close to the values of the Kingdom of God and those of the early Church.

5

Interfaith Dialogue in the Periphery

How to serve the poor and marginalized within the periphery?
How to learn from their social and religious experience? How
to deal with change and religious crisis? These seem to be challenging questions for today as they were challenging questions
before for Christians in Latin America. In May 2007 Benedict
XVI alerted the 430-strong group of Brazilian bishops that
there was a new crisis arising, that of the decrease of Catholic
identity and the following of 'sects', meaning Pentecostal movements.[150] Within some countries of Latin America up to 10 per
cent of Catholics have become evangelicals or Pentecostals
since the 1968 bishops' conference in Medellín and increasing
processes of secularism have expanded the possibilities that
people can openly say that they do not believe in God or simply
that they are spiritual but they do not associate their spiritual
quest with being part of a Christian church or a Christian community.[151] In Brazil, for example, the Catholic population has
fallen from 89 per cent in 1980 to 74 per cent today.[152]

Since the 1970s, the social concerns and the methodologies of
Latin American theology have been dominated by theological
developments within the Roman Catholic and to some extent
the Methodist churches but the phenomenon of evangelicals and
evangelism in general has been a peripheral issue within religious practices because religious practices within liberation
theology have been preoccupied with matters of religion and
politics, the practice of religion and the social concerns of localized communities. It is at the start of the twenty-first century that
the ongoing religious change in Latin America has prompted a
preoccupation with the conditions for a new Reformation, not

in Europe, where numbers of Christians are decreasing, but in the Americas where the majority of Christians of the world live. Even where the numbers of Pentecostals have increased they are still a minority vis-à-vis Roman Catholics. Nevertheless, Pentecostal churches and Pentecostal communities are particularly active within the poor areas of the urban centres of Latin America and they challenge the possibility of having a single centralized way of theologizing at the periphery. If during the time of the military regimes they could be ignored because, apart from the case of Guatemala, they didn't have any political power, within a twenty-first century process of theologizing in the periphery they cannot be ignored.

This chapter examines some of these changes in the theological outlook of contemporary Latin America and argues, following José Comblin and Leonardo Boff, that the changes cannot be met with intellectual paradigms such as the radical orthodoxy of John Milbank, but with an ongoing cooperation between the traditional churches and the Pentecostal churches within the periphery and by a process of challenging fundamentalism within all levels of religion and politics.[153] That cooperation, though, should continue to serve the poor and should leave the theological upper hand to the marginalized and their communities, to society's outcasts and their discourses, and should be firmly rooted in the values of the Kingdom of God as outlined in the Gospels through the actions of Jesus of Nazareth. Thus, a pluralistic interfaith theology for Latin America calls once again for a decentralization of ecclesiastical structures, Roman Catholic and Pentecostal, and for a hermeneutics of suspicion towards any established process that marginalizes the poor and the outcasts within contemporary Latin American society.

Social Change and Religious Crisis

Adolfo Nicolás SJ, referring primarily to the context of Christianity in Asia, has argued that 'crisis happens every time we open ourselves to the "others" and let our minds, hearts and imaginations be affected (enriched) by them'.[154] For Nicolás, Christianity in Asia has been in crisis since the arrival of the first missionaries. The same could be said of Latin America. At the beginning of 'the encounter' a colonial Christianity had to encounter the challenge of indigenous religions, and after the independence of the Latin American nations Christianity had to learn how to live within more secular societies where battles for education were not always easy. The period of the military regimes was indeed a great crisis whereby local Episcopal conferences had to decide how to respond to centralized dictatorial states and the systematic violation of human rights. Out of those periods of crisis Christianity grew stronger because it was able to adapt to changes and at the same time it was able to connect a Christian spirituality, a way of life, with the process of change and the actors within those periods within history.

However, here it must be remembered that the nature of the Church as an instrument of evangelization is to proclaim the Good News, not primarily to secure her future. Thus, the theological preoccupations within a changing Latin America need to be *ad extra*: to proclaim the Good News within the periphery, to accept that the poor and the marginalized have agency and that they theologize, and that the challenges faced by the traditional bases of liberation theology could and might lead to further liberation and further empowerment of the poor and the marginalized. For, after all, according to Eduardo de la Serna, 'the root of the crisis of Christianity is a crisis of *spirituality*, understanding the word in its sense of "journeying according to the spirit"'.[155] Liberation theology had already addressed those issues by connecting a liberating praxis with the possibility of being a Christian within society so that faith in God and love of neighbour became a united way of listening to the poor and the marginalized within society. However, for the majority of Christians in Latin America the fact that they were born Catholics meant in practice that few attended Sunday Mass and only a few took part in parish activities or belonged to the Basic Christian Communities. The crisis of spirituality still is a crisis of the Church that has failed to disentangle issues of power from issues of ongoing service and conversion. The Basic Christian Communities were able to rediscover the biblical text and to ask questions about their own way of life within the places where they lived rather than try to become individual saints responding to the grace of God and therefore being saved, saved without their community.

Throughout the period of the military regimes the theologizing by the Basic Christian Communities spoke of the temporal, of the material and of an incarnate God while the Pentecostal theologies with their public openness to human emotions emphasized a personal conversion from sin and a *doxa* of God that was somehow dissociated from daily life as far as social issues were concerned. The contemporary challenge is to carry on understanding different charismas and different traditions in relation to the option for the poor within the periphery rather than the inherent historical contradictions of the two different ways of being Christian in Latin America.

Interfaith Issues

If in Asia the theologizing is marked by an interfaith dialogue with the other world religions and in Africa Christianity has to deal with the ongoing practice of indigenous religions, the case of interfaith dialogue in Latin America points to a new path.[156] Traditional churches are not accustomed to dialogue and their clerical structures do not allow for that. The Second Vatican Council changed the situation of interfaith dialogue by welcoming Protestant observers to the council's proceedings and by encouraging a road towards Christian unity that over the years has been paved by ecumenical meetings and interfaith commissions.

I remember taking part in a couple of meetings of the Ecumenical Fraternity in the late 1970s in Chile, a meeting at which representatives of the traditional churches (Roman Catholic and Syrian Orthodox) and those that arose out of the Reformation (Presbyterian, Lutheran) met in order to discuss

common themes and to pray together. The meetings were con-
ducted with absolute respect for each others' traditions and
ended with tea and biscuits being served. They still seem to me
after all these years an isolated exercise triggered by the friend-
ships of individuals rather than meetings in which serious theological discussions could take place. What is clear though is that
Evangelicals and Pentecostals were not part of those meetings
supported by the Roman Catholic Archdiocese of Santiago.

That group had certainly been founded in order to follow the
instructions and the spirit of Vatican II's decree on ecumenism
(21 November 1964), a document that stated very clearly 'The
restoration of unity among all Christians is one of the principal
concerns of the Second Vatican Council. Christ the Lord
founded one Church and one Church only.'[157] Further, the
council distinguished between the division between churches of
the West and East and also between the Roman Catholic
Church and other churches after the European Reformation.
Use of and reverence for the Bible unites all these communities,
however, while it is clear that the authority of Scripture within
the Protestant churches is different from that within the Roman
Catholic Church, where 'its authentic teaching office has a
special place in expounding and preaching the written Word of
God'.[158]

If the Second Vatican Council encouraged ecumenical discussions between theologically educated groups, most of the good
will between the different Christian groups in Latin America
can be found in the mutual cooperation for the common good.
For example, after the Chilean military coup of September
1973 representatives from the different Christian churches
and the Jewish community sponsored a committee for peace
(COPACHI), a group that involved clerics, social workers and
lawyers, in order to support those political opponents of the
military regime who were suffering, together with their families. In those situations people of different Christian denomina-
tions come naturally together; it is only when undue pressure to
attend a particular church is shown that Christian groups dis-
pute each other's claims to 'truth' and 'salvation'. Within these

situations the poor and the marginalized are used to negotiating in their neighbourhoods between religious practices and ways of being Christian. The power of the Kingdom values remain part of a base not of a structure, so that the infrastructure can adapt while the superstructure becomes ever more isolated. Interfaith dialogue becomes an ongoing cooperation between the traditional churches and the new Pentecostalism in order to maintain the service and agency given to the poor by Jesus of Nazareth within the Gospels.

For a born-and-bred and practising Roman Catholic like myself this still sounds very strange but I follow the argument of theologizing from the periphery and, provided that the values of the Kingdom within the base of the poor are maintained, I am willing to follow the people's path and accept that God works in many ways and not only through one way of being Christian or one way of being human. José Comblin has emerged as one of those who believe that those who work within working-class districts of Latin America in particular would have no problem in working side by side with those who follow 'the new popular religion' and that the traditional churches will try to survive by allying themselves with the new phenomenon. Of course, Comblin's perspective has always been very pastoral and his ecumenical experience in Brazil and Chile has paved the way for a missiological approach of inclusion rather than exclusion. Thus, for Comblin, the varied manifestations of the Church are not of the essence of the gospel that 'remains hidden in the cracks of history'.[159]

For others, such as Leonardo Boff, Brazilians are 'natural syncretists' and the dialogue should be with indigenous religious traditions.[160] Regardless of that possibility and of the good relations between Christians and those who practise African religions in Brazil, the Pentecostal phenomenon has not been directly confronted by traditional churches. One of the difficulties is, of course, the fact that Pentecostal congregations do not necessarily have a defined structure comparable with that of other churches while, in the Chilean case, it has been possible for the different evangelical churches to come together under a larger umbrella of those who, rather than celebrating the sacraments, prefer to celebrate 'the flames of the Spirit'. There is no doubt that at the level of State–Church relations the Catholic Church has lost its centrality and that under equal opportunities legislation all churches and congregations that have acquired charity status have become part of the religious fibre of Latin America. This change, implemented in Chile by the government of President Bachelet in 2005, has made religious dialogue possible and the structure of congregations within the Latin American states possible.

However, intellectual dialogue between Roman Catholics and Pentecostals is not the way forward in my opinion. If those dialogues take place, different theologies would clash and a possible avenue of Christian witness to communal cooperation could be lost. Instead, at the periphery, all Christian churches need to cooperate as local communities in order to enhance their own lives in connection with a Latin American preferential option for the poor. After all, all Christian communities, be they Roman Catholic, Protestant or Pentecostal, are called to live the values of the gospel and to exercise the love of God and the love of neighbour. It is here, once again, that theological positions that emphasize orthodoxy and those that emphasize identity and belonging do not seem to work in the cooperative and communal efforts at applying the values of the Kingdom to ordinary life by all within a peripheral community, already excluded, already in need. In a different manner and in another context, Jürgen Manemann has expressed this reality by stating that 'for theology will not get to the "sources of the self" (Charles Taylor) by means of idealistic philosophies, but only when it speaks of everyday sufferings which are frequently hidden or written off as banal'.[161]

It is that ordinary experience that challenges the path of orthodoxy with orthopraxis and of self-identity with solidarity and a preferential option for the poor. This option leads to conversion and away from the problems of power that have managed to alter the right relation between the gospel and the Church during different periods of the history of Christianity.

Changing Theological Histories

There are two factors that remain problematic in any interfaith dialogue between the traditional churches and the Pentecostal movement in Latin America. The first one is certainly the free interpretation of the biblical text by which Pentecostal preachers adapt the actual demands of the gospel to a happy Good News with forthcoming prosperity and without the demands for social justice and communal peace that have been central to liberation theology and remain part of the Latin American preferential option for the poor. The second factor is the arrival of Pentecostal missionaries from the United States who do not adapt to the sociocultural structures of Latin America and therefore create a social break between those who are saved and those who remain sinners within one family. The 'gospel of prosperity' becomes an addictive message that allows numbers of converts to fill the Pentecostal churches but does not have an impact on local issues of poverty, marginalization and structural sin. Conversion is geared to the individual and remains within the realm of the individual, with an emotional burst of joy and happiness in which those who are sinners or belong to other churches are excluded.

For the Catholic Church this socioreligious change consti- tutes a crisis that has been triggered over the years by the overemphasis on the Church's structure and that in turn has impeded further indigenous ways of expression within the liturgy, particularly by Latin American indigenous communi- ties. The crisis in itself has been aggravated by the fact that ecumenical ties with other religious groups and a diversity of churches were made more difficult by documents such as *Dominus Iesus*, signed by Cardinal Ratzinger in 2000 with an overemphasis upon God's will to have one single Church, the Roman Catholic Church.[162] Thus, the demography and socio- religious relations within Latin American Christianity are changing, changes that at the moment cannot be evaluated in all their magnitude. There is no doubt that the theme of liberation unites the two major traditions on the ground, the Roman

Catholic and the Pentecostal, but with a general sense of a diverse understanding of sin and of belonging to a community. It is a fact that Benedict XVI was building bridges in his visit to Brazil in 2007 by emphasizing a more individualistic approach to sin and to conversion, an approach that can persuade Catholics and Pentecostals that they are journeying in the same way to the Kingdom. At the same time, the classification of Pentecostal communities as 'sects' does not help matters. The term seems to have been inherited from previous documents prepared by the Latin American bishops, for example, the final document of Santo Domingo, but 'sect' would not be commonly used in Europe or North America where some of these groups would be called evangelicals and others born-again Christians.[163]

The diversity of religious practices within a Latin America of the twenty-first century does not resemble a crisis of spirituality or a crisis of faith. On the contrary, most Christians in the world still live in Latin America and most of them are happy within their ongoing religious practice, a less intellectual practice of religion than in Europe.[164] The crisis is of religious change, and the interests of the different groups involved in preserving or acquiring spheres of influence within the nation state can trigger the possibility of forgetting the poor and the marginalized. Sobrino's response to crises stands as a relevant one for all the Christian traditions because it goes back to the kenosis, to the emptying of God, God already appearing defenceless in our midst like one of us. Thus, Sobrino writes:

> What can we do about these crises, if God is in the midst of them? Faced with the crisis of 'sacramentality', there remain conversion and being and acting like Jesus. Faced with the crisis of 'religion', there remains integrity with reality, living *etsi religio non daretur*. Faced with the crisis of God, there remains returning to the sorrow and the love of the world, to the passion and love of God.[165]

The relocation of the traditional and Pentecostal churches must be towards the periphery and here is where liberationists and urban Pentecostals meet. In a previous encounter the liberationists were very critical of the military regimes while the Pentecostals supported them. With the military out of the way the scenario remains that of democratic and secularized societies where the social forces within the State are constituted by civil society and not by the churches. Therefore, a model of cooperation between all the churches requires an immersion in the community projects of the periphery rather than the isolated efforts of a particular Christian group or Christian denomination. A spirituality of solidarity with the poor and not with any kind of cultural Christianity remains the way ahead, along with an authoritative way of reading Scripture by a community that journeys as a body rather than as isolated individuals who want to be saved without caring about others, particularly the most vulnerable within society.

Towards an Interreligious Theology

I am the first one to recognize the difficulties arising out of a possible theological dialogue between Roman Catholicism and Pentecostalism. However, I am also conscious that great cooperation and theological understanding between Catholic and Protestant Latin American theologians came about because of their love for people and their challenge to the State that didn't provide the means for human existence for all within the Latin American nation state. I am hopeful that any decentralization towards the periphery creates the possibility for a common search, even when at times the theological language of both sides is completely contradictory. I am hopeful that a decentralization of Christianity for the sake of survival would create the conditions for a theologizing from the underside of history that would include all those peripheries and places of exclusion that do not have a voice. Thus, while I remain centred within a particular form of Christianity, I once again stress the centrality of the Kingdom of God as an all-embracing contemporary and future reality in which the reign of God would take precedence with a clear mapping of social and individual attitudes towards material things, wealth, riches and power, as outlined by the ministry of Jesus of Nazareth.

An interreligious theology assumes not a relativistic position but the possibility that a theologian as an interpreter of God's actions does not possess all the truth and the fullness of revelation. That truth in Christianity comes from Christ; and the churches, as instruments of Christ, serve as means of salvation so that the people of God form a community rather than a group of isolated individuals. According to the Second Vatican Council:

> At all times and in every race, anyone who fears God and does what is right has been acceptable to him (cf. Acts 10:35). He has, however, willed to make men holy and save them, not as individuals without any bond or link between them, but rather to make them into a people who might acknowledge him and serve him in holiness.[166]

The theological difficulties between the traditional churches in Latin America and the arising Pentecostalism relate to different general understandings of sin, of liturgical rites and of the interpretation of the Christian Scriptures. One can say that the use of the biblical text unites people at the periphery because the emphasis on the need to read the Scriptures in community and as individuals by the Latin American bishops has matched the Pentecostals' zeal for reading the Scriptures. However, one of the most difficult parts of the inter-theological and inter-religious dialogue is the understanding of the social, of the world around us, of the humanly made structures that mediate people's democratic wishes and democratic institutions in Latin America. According to Comblin:

> Pentecostal churches condemn the world and all worldly activities; they condemn economics, politics, and culture because everything is contaminated with sin, and everything is idolatry. They accordingly proclaim that this world is ending and the reign of God is coming soon. They assume no

responsibility for this world that has abandoned God and that God has abandoned.[167]

Comblin's assessment stands true for many of the small Christian congregations that associated with the Baptism movement that came and went in many different neighbourhoods of Latin America. However, the Pentecostal movement has a more structured and more foreign-influenced policy and therefore theology. The worldliness of the newly arising Pentecostalism relates to a neoliberal evangelical theology of prosperity directly associated with capitalism and with the neoconservatism prevailing within the administration of President George W. Bush. The 'gospel of prosperity' has made Pentecostalism a powerful force among those who lack everything because it has given them an identity and a hope that other religious organizations cannot offer. Thus, if the poor hear about a theology centred on the value of poverty they acquire a certain social identity; however, if they hear statements regarding hopes and material opportunities they jump at the chance and we cannot blame them.

However, one could argue that the image of Pentecostalism during the military regimes has tinted the liberationist view of them. For the beginnings of Pentecostalism were among the oppressed and the social outcasts. The recognized founder of Pentecostalism was William Joseph Seymour (1870–1922), a son of former slaves from Centerville, Louisiana, and a student in Charles Fox Parham's Bible School in Topeka, Kansas. Parham was a sympathizer of the Ku Klux Klan and therefore excluded Seymour from entering the room but allowed him to listen to the Bible lessons. Later, Seymour received the baptism of the Spirit and moved to Los Angeles, where he started a revivalist movement and taught in a Holiness church.[168] The Los Angeles revival of 1906 is considered the cradle of Pentecostalism, a phenomenon by which a group of Black Americans introduced Negro spirituals into their worship, allowed participants to speak in tongues and introduced a new meaning of Pentecost. According to Walter Hollenweger:

It meant loving in the face of hate – overcoming the hatred of a whole nation by demonstrating that Pentecost is something very different from the success-oriented American way of life.[169]

Both Seymour and Parham remain at the heart of historical Pentecostalism but they represent two different theological strands: Parham emphasized speaking in tongues while Seymour emphasized the unity of the believer with the Spirit and the healing of the nations. Thus, the road from the religious practices of the marginalized to those of an institutionalized middle class in Pentecostalism can be compared with the same phenomenon in Roman Catholicism. Both fight for the heart of the poor within Latin America because one offers human dignity to the believer (Catholicism) while the other offers individual identity and self-expression (Pentecostalism), sometimes absent from the Roman liturgical rite in its traditional celebration, and a prospect of a social identity, an important marker of sociability within contemporary Latin America.[170] Both traditions face the challenge of returning to their roots and their understanding of a message of unity among peoples with the 'tongues of fire' or without them.[171] Most importantly for an age of globalization, both traditions have become global and transnational traditions of Christianity.[172]

Historically and at the time of Vatican II there were ecumenical conversations between Roman Catholics and Pentecostals, and later the Catholic Charismatic Renewal Movement arose out of the possibility of a self-expression in worship that was previously absent in the Tridentine Rite of the Mass. However, the two strands that publicly could be deemed compatible expressed two different theologies, a community of the Spirit within Catholicism and an individual baptism of the Spirit within Pentecostalism. Later, Pentecostals joined prayer meetings of the Catholic Pentecostals in Europe and a series of ecumenical meetings took place sponsored by the Vatican between Pentecostal scholars and Catholic scholars. They were not publicized because of the fear by the participants of being challenged by their own communities. They discussed themes such as 'Baptism in the Spirit', 'Receiving the Spirit and Christian Regeneration', 'Spiritual Gifts', 'Public Worship', 'Discernment' and 'Prayer and Praise'.[173] The first series of meetings took place between 1972 and 1976 with locations as varied as Zurich (1972), Rome (1973), Craheim in Germany (1974), Venice (1975) and Rome (1976). Further meetings took place in Rome (1977 and 1979), Venice (1980), Vienna (1981) and Collegeville, Minnesota (1982). After the election of John Paul II a new series of meetings was planned and took place in Riano in Italy (1985), Venice (1987), Emmetten in Switzerland (1988) and Rome (1989) with the writing of a final report. The debates were at times difficult, especially when discussing baptism, ecclesiology and the papacy. However, those discussions show that a Catholic–Pentecostal dialogue has already taken place and that it is certainly possible within Latin America.

Other scholarly works such that of Chan on Pentecostal theology and the Christian spiritual tradition have shed light on areas of Pentecostal theology vis-à-vis Roman Catholic theology where more work needs to be done. The Church assumes within Pentecostalism a weak sociological sense and baptism is understood as an individual's saving moment that creates a different ecclesial understanding than the Body of Christ assumed by Roman Catholics as a sociological body that incorporates those who have been received into the Church as the Body of Christ. Instead, the Body of Christ for Pentecostal theology 'means that in God's economy of redemption, he called people from the old creation and reconstituted them a new creation in Christ'.[174] The Pentecostal model of church is weak in that it cares for personal salvation at the expense of the community: 'all too often, Pentecostals are more concerned with their "personal Pentecost" than with the corporate Pentecostal reality of which each person has a share'.[175] Other differences relate to baptism and the priesthood of all believers as well as members of a Pentecostal community vis-à-vis the salvation of others. It is important, in my opinion, to record these complexities within the history of theology in Latin America and to return to avenues of shared experience and differences between the diverse elements of Christianity in Latin America in future research.

The complexity is astonishing because there are Pentecostals who value some aspects within the fight against unjust structures and as a matter of fact some Pentecostals supported the Sandinista government in Nicaragua, the socialist government of Salvador Allende in Chile and even the membership of Pentecostal groups within the World Council of Churches. In response to criticisms about Pentecostalism's lack of commitment to the liberation of the oppressed and the poor Cecilia Loreto Maríz stated the following:

> The Catholic Church opts for the poor because it is not a church of the poor. Pentecostal churches do not opt for the poor because they are already a poor people's church and that is why the poor people are opting for them.[176]

Further, Latin American Pentecostals have been at the forefront of ecumenical relations in general and dialogue with Roman Catholicism in particular. Among the personalities involved, one could mention the Chilean Pentecostal Marta Palma, formerly in charge of the Latin American and Caribbean desk on human rights of the World Council of Churches.[177] The Pentecostals face the same theological challenges over Eurocentrism and the actual marginalization of Latin American theologians on the ground. Their theological agreements are still in progress, however, so that sometimes it is difficult to see the influence of Latin American Pentecostalist theologians within the wider globalized picture. There is a further investigation on these ecumenical relations that is wider than this work, however, full of promise rather than an antagonistic labelling of Church and 'sects'. Thus, I fully agree with a leading scholar on Pentecostalism when he concludes one of his seminal books with the following remarks:

If Pentecostals and Catholics, independents and Anglicans, Methodists and charismatics, Presbyterians and 'non-white indigenous churches' dig deep enough into their own traditions, they might discover some considerable common ground (both of content and of form) for a global system of cooperation and communication. This, it seems to me, is as necessary for the world and the church as is our daily bread.[178]

With such sociotheological reality in mind it is possible to argue that the possible theological dialogue and encounter could take place within the periphery as Pentecostals become more involved in social issues and Catholics become more involved in 'the life of the Spirit'. Thus, the power of religious pluralism could become once again a prophetic sign of challenges by the infrastructure towards the superstructure within nation states and within the churches. The poor and the marginalized then can become agents of pluralism and of the work of the Spirit within a periphery where diversity is the norm and orthodoxy part of the centre's thirst for power and control. It is to these processes of diversity or the absence of it that Leonardo Boff refers when he argues that we live in an age of fundamentalisms: 'we are lacerated by radicalisms, unilateralist positions, fundamentalisms and nonsensical polarizations in almost all fields'.[179] Maybe Latin America can become the peripheral place for a diversified, interfaith and interreligious theological praxis that could show the future, and contemporary realities, of the Kingdom of God or, in the words of José María Vigil, 'share what emerges in common: an "interreligious theology" of liberation'.[180] Maybe the acceptance of theological finitude and of humble theologizing could also help a theologizing within the periphery or, in the more creative terms of Marcelo Barros, accepting a 'hiero-diversity', thus 'accepting that our theology and our discourse about God are partial and incomplete'.[181]

We also live in an age of consumerism, and the possibility of solidarity with the periphery as well as the fact that there is not enough to eat or basic human rights within the periphery challenges the theologizing of a Christianity that in becoming established has become comfortable and acceptable. In the next chapter I examine some of the possible values of the Kingdom of God that challenge an established sense of Christianity and I argue for a more radical lifestyle, always at the periphery and always challenging the neo-colonialism of acquired habits from the US empire.

6

Poverty and Consumerism

So much theologizing at the periphery of Latin America became connected to the materially poor that casuistic European theological questions concentrated on the nature of the poor rather than on the gospel call to poverty and to a Christian life that spoke of the values of the Kingdom. Latin American theology was seen as a political and economic system rather than as a renewal of Christian values and a new contextual hermeneutics arising not out of social theory but from the gospel while using social theory in order to understand the social processes of injustice and oppression within contemporary Latin American society. Among those who concentrated their efforts on a personal and community life of poverty were Franciscan theologians and their associations: for example: Leonardo Boff focused on the life and ideals of St Francis of Assisi.[182] Others connected the monastic ideals of poverty to their own Christian discipleship/way of life and as a result to their own theologizing: Ernesto Cardenal, for example, started a monastic community, thus a life of holding property in common, in Solentiname, Nicaragua, searching for God and challenging the materialism of Nicaraguan society.[183] In any reading of the Gospels as I attempted in Chapter 2, above, it becomes clear that poverty is closer to the gospel while riches and human attachment to them become a hindrance for any followers of Jesus of Nazareth throughout the New Testament.[184]

In this chapter I explore the value of a life of poverty as a Christian choice and as a sign of the Kingdom, and consumerism and the associated dehumanizing practices as anti-values vis-à-vis Christianity and therefore not conducive to Christian liberation or to a theologizing that comes out of the poor and the marginalized. Further, I argue that consumerism contributes to the oppression of the poor because it exalts the value of the market rather than of a common humanity.

Theologizing Commonality

In between challenges of activism and theologizing at the periphery there are central statements that are forgotten or are taken for granted, and they remain unspoken. One of them was highlighted by the Dalai Lama in his Nobel Prize Lecture (1989) when he opened the solemn occasion with the following remark:

> I am always reminded that we are all basically alike: we are all human beings. Maybe we have different clothes, our skin is of a different colour, or we speak different languages. This is on the surface. But basically, we are the same human beings. That is what binds us to each other.[185]

Latin American theology has followed that pattern of commonality by centring action and reflection within history, rather than centring the process of theologizing within the individual.[186] The comparison with other faiths and with other modes of being is striking because in an individualistic mode the person as individual makes history without depending on others. However, for theologizing at the periphery where lesser material means are available there is a need for cooperation and a certain dependency on others. With that cooperation in mind and that life of community at the centre it is possible to respond to the central calling: that of the Spirit. Jon Sobrino has summarized that calling and that questioning in a very dramatic way, as dramatic as Sobrino's life in Central America, in the following words:

> What are you, and what ought you to be? What do you hope

for, and what might you hope for? What are you doing, and what should you be doing? What are you celebrating, and what could you be celebrating? From out of the midst of history itself, the call has sounded: Answer for the truth of history truthfully. Shape that history, do not be dominated by it or merely slip and slide passively through it.[187]

There is an inherent contradiction and a creative one within the life of the periphery and any life of poverty: poverty is not willed by God on any human being. But when someone is no longer poor there is a need to remember poverty as a value because God opts for the poor and the marginalized.[188] In other words, there are further theological distinctions regarding the issue of poverty and the life of poverty:

1. there are those who do not choose material poverty,
2. there are those who choose poverty as a gospel value and follow a particular way of life such as the monastic or religious life,
3. there are those who strive to do well but are content with a simple style of life, and
4. there are those who strive to do better and never achieve a personal contentment with what they have, even when their situation is materially better than (1), (2) or/and (3).

Theologizing on the periphery provides a challenge to all these groups of people in their common humanity because it allows the centrality of community and the centrality of the gospel to mirror other possibilities of existence. There is no linear progression, as within developmental economics, between poverty and riches, between closeness to the gospel and the hardening of hearts through riches, but instead there is a circular reality, that of the Kingdom of God, that embraces all those realities as centred upon the values of the Kingdom of God. This creates a double principle: an ethical one to live according to the values of the Kingdom and a hermeneutical one that requires action in order to learn the values of the Kingdom.[189]

As a result of those ethical and hermeneutical considerations the contemporary process of theologizing in Latin America and elsewhere requires both an ethical and a hermeneutical response, both responses supported by a spirituality, by a way of life in which the Spirit of God reinforces the necessary graces and understandings of history so as to trigger theologizing at the periphery from the point of view of the poor and the marginalized.[190]

Market versus Person

One of the most challenging experiences of my visits to North America has been the visits to shopping malls. Shopping has become a way of life for some and at the same time a way of relating for others. Shopping in general and shopping malls in particular are not bad; however, they are the reflection of a human experience dictated by the market in which personal satisfactions arise out of a relation through things rather than through human attitudes. 'Are you coming?' and 'We are going shopping?' become not questions about a human need for food, clothing or human pleasure in which, because an item is needed, there is the need to go to a place where one can get it, but a reflection on the self, the human and the divine all together. Without realizing, some, if not many human beings, start relating to each other through what they have and how they look. Here, I express my deep ongoing satisfaction with a well-dressed person at any time; I am speaking of a phenomenon where human time and human self are defined by the market rather than by human relations; I am speaking about the need to spend. At its worst a human being goes to the mall in case there is anything interesting and returns with items that are not needed or not wanted. Therefore, my theologizing about the shopping mall does not exclude the usefulness and even possible architectural beauty of a mall but the fact that human beings can substitute relatedness and human creativity for shopping and having. Two examples illustrate the substitution of a creative human activity for a material inclusion in a world fabricated by the market and by those who control the market through the media.

The first example is the creative theologizing of Ola Sigurdson, who in her insightful analysis of pop music and God has argued that 'with regard to the question of God in pop-music I suggest that the common denominator is the quest for what it means to be an authentic human being' and that 'this quest often – not always – calls upon God or some higher spiritual being for help'.[191] Indeed, human creativity and the presence of God as beauty or companion of beauty are themes that have inspired the great cathedrals of Europe and the great musicians of church music and some of the pop music composers. It is a pleasure and a divine extension of eternal beauty when one listens to music that one enjoys. However, shopping as a human activity can relate to the possibility of listening to music, to the actual shopping at the mall or to any shopping via the internet. In so far as the shopping is controlled and creates beauty it is part of a human creative activity in which the rested human spirit can dwell on the refreshing notes of an activity that enhances the senses, the spirit and the communal sense of beauty. If that shopping for pop music becomes an activity in its own right rather than the music then one is referring to a process of consumerism in which buying, having and consuming become the objective rather than the human activity of enjoying music.

The second example is the idea sold by the market that a common humanity, globalization and economic development relate to the possibility that all peoples in the world can drink Coca-Cola, can wear blue jeans and can use the internet in order to feel part of one world. The market has pushed hard through the media that idea of inclusion, an idea that collapses by the time that members of the Empire are drinking Coca-Cola at your doorsteps or when the poor and marginalized are turned away from a national frontier because they have the wrong nationality, the wrong papers or the wrong intentions. Those rejected at a border can still go away and drink Coca-Cola but they are not able to convince the officials who guard the wall that separates the United States and Mexico that they are both equal in a world of a common humanity and common universal rights, in which humanity is divided between those who create and open the markets and the rest, the recipients of those ideas and market practices.

The market exists, and a process of theologizing asks questions about God and about human beings in relation rather than sanctioning the possibility of the existence of financial institutions and their policies. It is through that theologizing that a third part of the hermeneutical circle, the excluded, join the shopper and the seller at the market of the shopping mall. If there are significant numbers of human beings who cannot have enough to eat or who fail to acquire their basics needs, is it possible for an honest Christianity to continue consuming rather than being? My answer is a categorical 'no' and the close reading of the Gospels points to the same message. There is a direct relation between the following of God and the compassion for the poor and there is a direct connection between centring on the periphery and the demands for a simpler life, for poverty of the spirit, and for a constant preoccupation for other human beings. It is here that the scandal of the consumerist world appears, because the values of the Kingdom of God through equality for all human beings disappear.

If the worth of a human being is what the person can acquire through shopping then there are more important human beings: those who shop better acquire goods that attract attention and have a large home so as to be able to store those hundreds of items. Instead, if one follows the values of the Kingdom all human beings have the same worth and within those human beings God takes immediate and more intensive care of the poor and the marginalized; God loves a human being and all human beings regardless of their possibilities at shopping and their prosperity and within those human beings God is closer to those who take care of other human beings and those who have put their heart in God rather than in material possessions. Further, as pointed out by William Cavanaugh, the celebration of God's Kingdom by the community, that is, in the Eucharist, 'places judgement in the eschatological context of God's inbreaking Kingdom' so that 'the Kingdom is not driven by our desires but by God's desire which we receive as gift in the Eucharist'.[192]

One of the difficulties in Latin America as expressed through many theological writings is the ever-growing division between the poor and the rich, between those under or just above the poverty line and those who have more and more and are able to become successful consumers.[193] The difficulty is not only financial but spiritual. It is financial because there are millions of human beings who cannot feed their families, have access to primary education or clean water, but it is spiritual because it is very clear that the message of the gospel which has been accepted by the majority of Latin Americans does not make any difference in most of the policies and social approaches to basic human rights. During the period of the military regimes, it was possible to blame the armies for spending most of a country's financial assets on defence and the fighting of insurgents; under the democracies there is nobody to blame but the elected politicians, the majority of whom profess allegiance to the Christian faith and have been in the past victims of human rights abuses.

Poverty and Beatitude

It is here that one looks for the possibility of spiritual centres of change and of Christian commitment within the Latin American nations. Throughout the history of the Church and throughout the development of Christianity in Latin America the monasteries of contemplatives, men and women, have reminded us of the values of the Kingdom in a way that sometimes the structures of the churches have not.[194] Monasteries are located at the periphery because of the monks' search for solitude, silence and God outside the noisy urban places where the shopping malls are located.

The centre of the monastic life relates to activities that are constant, daily routines of prayer, work and communal meals together with a repeated reading of the Scriptures in community, the search for a communal poverty, and a daily search for the voice of God within the walls of the monastery.[195] The monasteries are places of subversion and transgression because they refuse the possible acceptance of values outside the Kingdom and they do not comply with secular life or even with ecclesiastical structures as the head of an abbey, the Abbot, acts as a bishop towards the community, without having to comply with the pastoral plans of the diocese in which they are located. Monasteries are signs of non-compliance and of the possibility of liberation from consumerism and from the slavery of the market. Monasteries are places where the Kingdom of God is proclaimed as master of all other political systems, the master of consumerism and the master of other processes associated with the centre.[196] The care of the poor and sometimes the defence of the poor are associated with ways in which men and women of courage proclaim that the King is still to come and that not everything is well in the contemporary world.

It is not by chance that there is a close connection between prayer, contemplation, mysticism, actions for peace and actions for non-violence.[197] There is, for example, a historical connection between the influence of Thomas Merton, Trappist monk, writer and political activist who lived at the Abbey of Our Lady of Gethsemani in Kentucky, USA, on Ernesto Cardenal and the later Trappist foundation in Santiago, Chile.[198] If Merton supported the peace movement of the 1960s from his enclosure, he also encouraged Cardenal to go ahead with the monastic foundation at Solentiname, Nicaragua. To make matters ever more transgressive the monks of Santiago helped some of the politicians who had served under Salvador Allende's government by hiding them from Pinochet's security forces in the hermitage of their monastery.[199]

I am not advocating here that every Christian in Latin America should become a monk but I am pointing to the fact that the increase in consumerism is countered by the spiritual lives of those who, guided by a simple life, challenge the values of the market and consumerism. By their actions they make political statements that follow the values of the Kingdom rather than the values of a secular or an unjust state that oppresses the poor. I am certainly pointing to a certain style of life that has been the mark and trade of theologians, revolutionaries and utopian people who have realized that their lifestyle should match their attitudes to daily life.

Theologizing against consumerism and with the poor and the marginalized takes a particular choice of lifestyle (see Chapter 9). Without that theological consciousness there is no hope of being there with the poor, for without a lifestyle that challenges the values of the market there is no chance of acquiring the values of the Kingdom. The soft approach to spirituality is certainly not part of the life of the poor who struggle with inner strength through the difficulties of daily life. Thus, since the fourth century, monks have struggled with the institutional powers and already the Donatists, condemned as heretics, could be considered the first Marxists within the history of the Church because they challenged the lifestyle and centrality of Rome and the new Christian emperor and quarrelled with Augustine about an established Christianity that for them had too many traits and too many functionaries who had evolved into functionaries of the Church from the former Roman Empire.

The monk is a revolutionary within Latin American theology because he is able to challenge the easy life of the market and becomes active as a constant bridge between the human and the divine, the social and the monastic.[200] In 1978, I had the chance to spend a few days on retreat at the Trappist monastery in Santiago and I was struck by the fact that the monks' work on the farm was very hard, that their habits were not as elegant as those of the Benedictines (later I learned that the Trappists have a more strict way of life than that of the Benedictines) and – most important – that the community was well aware of what was happening outside the walls as their bidding prayers throughout the daily offices and at the daily Eucharist requested protection for the persecuted, courage for the Church and solidarity with those who had asked for their prayers and their protection. The liturgical act of praise towards God was also a political act of theologizing action and society's needs. Their early prayer at 3:15 a.m. in the morning reminded me of a larger reality in which they were not escaping from the world of the poor and the marginalized. On the contrary, they had become a sign and challenge against injustice by just being there – a physical thorn in the flesh of the urban centre, reminding the world that utopia could exist and that the tentacles of power and greed could not have the last say. It is no surprise to me that the monks always had a flow of Chilean vocations, particularly among those who had been socially and politically very active.

A lifestyle that relates to the Beatitudes provides a sign of the Kingdom that challenges the market; it prepares those who are going through actions of theologizing, be they helping or living among the poor or taking part in political protests of non-violence against the State. A lifestyle that asks how much is too much and how God comes into every social and financial action creates solidarity with the poor that comes from the deeply rooted gospel action of uttering the Beatitudes. 'Blessed are the poor!' expresses exclusion for those who oppress the poor and who use the message of the gospel to pacify protests in order to sustain their power and their greed. 'Blessed' are those who choose to challenge the riches of this world because they prefer to ally with the poor, with God and with his Kingdom. 'Blessed' are the monks who challenge the possibility that the market controls time because through their ongoing marking of the hours through prayer and work they sanctify the hours with values of solidarity, community and divine violence. 'Blessed' are those who reject the possibility that human beings could become better by what they have; instead, they are ready to embrace all human beings, particularly those who cry because they have been evicted from their lands or those who have been bombed because they impeded the exploitation of oil and resources for the killing machines of the US empire.

A Spirituality of Transgression

The style of life of the periphery is marked by a spirituality of liberation, the liberation of oneself from the slavery of consumerism and the recognition that God works through the poor in the liberation of those oppressed within contemporary society. In the words of Pedro Casaldáliga and José María Vigil:

> We believe that today, in creative fidelity to this living tradition, we are called to live contemplation in liberative activity (*contemplativus in liberatione*), decoding surroundings made up of grace and sin, light and shade, justice and injustice, peace and violence, discovering in this historical process of liberation the presence of the Wind that blows where it will, uncovering and trying to build salvation history in the one history, finding salvation in liberation.[201]

Thus, within a contemplative tradition and within Latin American theology, spirituality, previously associated with pious practices and little action, becomes the action of the Spirit through a person who, within the periphery, acts on behalf of the poor and continues building up a liberating consciousness by a daily following of a lifestyle that connects with the values of the Kingdom of God and by a daily conversation with the God of Life, following the example of Jesus of Nazareth. Spirituality becomes in this way of life a life of transgression because the freedom of the Spirit means that such a person is not always complying with the rules of the market, the rule of the State, the rules of the Church or the rules of the monastery. Indeed, Thomas Merton had enormous problems with his abbot because the abbot didn't understand the fact that a monk was a writer, a political activist, a personal confidant and an interfaith activist all at the same time. There is no doubt that within the deepest disagreements between Merton and his abbot Merton spent longer periods in contemplation and for years became a solitary hermit in order to continue searching for the will of God as he continued corresponding with hundreds of people, including activists against the Vietnam War and even Buddhist philosophers.

The style of life that challenges the values of the unjust is a style of life that bears witness to the poverty of Jesus of Nazareth and declares openly the foolishness and injustice that creates multinational companies and financial wealth for the so-called billionaires of this world at the expense of the Third World and the poor of this world. Such a lifestyle becomes a continuation of a line of adherence to the gospel commitment to the poor throughout the centuries, starting with the Peruvian Saint Martin de Porres in colonial times and the development of monasteries in the twentieth century.

Transgression and theological transgressions at the periphery are a way of theologizing because, as in the case of the monk, they are signs of a world to come 'not yet' but 'here now'. Theological transgressions remain prophetic when they are able to recognize the centrality of the poor and of the Kingdom even if there are contradictions in such theologizing with the contemporary realities of a particular tradition or a particular church. The act of transgression is the unity of hunger and poverty at the periphery not only in spirit and desire but also in form, matter and lifestyle. Theological transgressions such as those explored by Marcella Althaus-Reid within theology and sexuality are also explorations that conduce to ethical responsibilities that arise not out of unchangeable norms but of social relations and the realities of a common humanity. Therefore, 'the perceived excessive consumerism and carelessness of some sections of the population is seen as sinful by destitute people who do not understand why things (in this case, discarded goods) are not shared with the community'.[202]

A simpler style of life for those who have more and a richer style of life for the poor is the way forward, with two provisos. The first one is that we become aware that the media and the market play with our desires for consumption. We are told that the more growth in the economy through our consumption the more jobs that could be created the more prosperity we could enjoy and the happier we would be. This is a false strategy because an increased consumption by us does not solve the breach between the rich and the poor or, in other words, 'self-interested consumption does not bring justice to the hungry' but 'consumerism is the death of Christian eschatology'.[203] Second, the search for the other is what drives our lives in the periphery for, if consumption allows a non-human exchange of desire and eventually kills it, the search for the other as co-human and as my own responsibility becomes a sign of the Kingdom. The prophets of the Kingdom are certainly those that in Latin America drive others to desire the values of the Kingdom; in the words of Hadwig Ana Maria Müller, 'they approach others not as rich people who have something to give but as those who are poor and want to receive from others. They do not suppress their search for relationships; they keep alive their desire, the hunger, within them.'[204]

It is here that common humanity and Christian eschatology meet because if Latin American theology has become a well-known global phenomenon within Christian theological circles it has been because of the challenges it posed to the US empire in the times of the Reagan administration and later through the cooperation between Latin American theologians and other Third World theologians. In questions of lifestyle and spirituality, I am tempted to argue that the future would need a further globalization of a Latin American spirituality because, in matters of poverty, hunger, emptiness, longing, enlightenment, submission, Kingdom values, anti-poverty, relatedness, otherness, contemplation and non-violence, a further cooperation is needed between Latin American theologians and the theologizing at the periphery with the theologizing of the oriental peripheries of a globalized world. Ernesto Cardenal was challenged by Thomas Merton's experience of the East in the 1960s and 1970s; is it not the time for a new and fresh encounter between Latin American theologians, theologizing at the periphery and Buddhism, particularly Tibetan Buddhism with its sense of exile and being on the periphery? Is it not the time to explore the sense of creation and ecological issues with Hinduism, particularly through the Hindu masters' understanding of their sacred

scriptures? Is it not the time to theologize with other peripheries
of the world in order to hear God's Kingdom at work? My
answer is an unequivocal 'yes' to those dialogues and the search
for a preferential option for the poor that becomes inclusive
rather than exclusive and that relates the injustice and oppression of human beings in Latin America, Africa and Asia. This
kind of opening to a cosmic theologizing was already stated by
the Association of Third World Theologians meeting in Mexico
in 1986 but has not been properly followed up from the point
of view of dialogue between Latin American theologians and
the world religions. It is understandable that matters of hunger,
injustice and poverty come first. The de-colonizing of other
beliefs and other cultures by Christianity needs to be addressed
as a matter of urgency, however, following the rich theological
statement of the final document of that conference:

> Jesus reveals God, but does not limit or exhaust the divine. In
> the light of the risen Jesus and the cosmic Christ, nothing pre-
> vents God's self-revelation to all God's people. It is liberating
> to confess that God is not confined to Christian traditions,
> churches, and scriptures. Wherever God makes self-disclo-
> sure and self-gift, the word enters the earth, becomes em-
> bodied in history, participates in people's struggles for justice
> and freedom, and helps propel them toward their (up)rising
> and liberation.[205]

I must admit that I have found enormous inspiration by
connecting the values of the Kingdom of God as a globalized
reality, by theologizing with those who follow other faiths, in
the Gospels as well as in the sayings of the Buddha, in the poetry
of Ernesto Cardenal as well as in the writings of the Dalai Lama,
in the compassion exalted in the *Bhagavat gita* or the Koran,
values that in the search of a spirituality of justice and compassion for the world challenge consumerism and the possibility
of a world and a Latin American society that does not care
for justice and peace. The signs of the Kingdom through the
contemporary experiences of monasticism, mysticism and con-

templation challenge the media's assumption that we are all consumers and that we are happy to consume. I am not a happy shopper; I enjoy the fruits of the earth, a good glass of wine with fellow travellers and an oily chicken stew in the periphery. At the end of the day I would always argue that the future of humanity and the presence of the God of Life lies at that globalized periphery where not only enemies would cease to fight each other, where the machines of war would be dismantled, where the US empire would cease to understand the world of God in terms of power and where Christians, Buddhists, Hindu and Muslims would live together under the umbrella of the values of the Kingdom within a globalized world that is just and in peace because every single human being has decided that it should be so.

It is possible to argue that history repeats itself and that the challenges of the 1960s are still with us, or they have returned unsolved. There is a 'war on terror'; poverty is still an issue that divides protestors, Christian activists and the leaders of the G-8 nations; secularism and freedom of conscience are at our doorsteps; millions still follow religious and ritual lives within the world religions; and Gutiérrez's assessment of Latin America still stands – it is a continent in which the realities of injustice and poverty are central to any understanding of the possibilities and impossibilities of a theologizing in which the Kingdom of God is here but not yet, a continent in which God is present:

> On this continent hope is born in the midst of suffering; it takes the form of life that comes through death. Its ultimate motivation is found in the living God, the God of tender love, who stoops to us in our suffering, our faith, and our efforts to be in solidarity with the Latin American poor and to win their liberation.[206]

In the next chapter I examine the possibilities of a theologizing with Latin America as part of a globalized community and the possible theological responses to these contemporary processes, not necessarily new in form but with new empires, new gods and new challenges for contemporary Latin American theologies.

Part 3

Theology and Activism

7

A Globalized Periphery

In the previous chapter I examined some pressing and ethical issues regarding consumerism, monasticism and lifestyles within Latin America. If the option for the poor is an ethical and Christian option for solidarity with those who are marginalized it is also an option to mediate between the realities of globalization and the periphery. The periphery, central to the Kingdom of God and its fulfilment, remains outside the maps of a globalized market economy because the periphery does not offer a real market for goods to be consumed, discarded and consumed again. In this chapter I want to explore three possibilities for a Latin American way of life within the periphery: (1) a model of compliance; (2) a model of rejection; and (3) a model of hermeneutical suspicion. It is my argument that neither a full compliance nor a full rejection of globalization is a social experience that connects with the values of the Kingdom or with the experience of the Church and that a model of critical-hermeneutical engagement could be the best possible response by the churches and by the periphery. However, this is a very complex mediation that requires the possibility of non-exclusion of the periphery's agency, knocking at the doors of the centres but happy to return to the periphery.

Globalized Realities

The churches, and particularly the Roman Catholic Church, are not strangers to globalized modes of existence. Globalization, a term that we have learned to use for conversational purposes and to blame for any social or other ills within the contemporary world, has been given an agency that even in a literary sense does not make sense. Living creatures have agency to move and to affect others by their lives and by their movements, even the smallest cell has some influence on others. However, globalization does not; it is human beings that have the agency to operate globalized processes and human beings are affected by those same processes of larger international negotiations, movements and new modes of existence.

In his latest work on globalization, Leonardo Boff has relied for his argument on the impact of technologies on the world, an argument that even before the creation of the internet or the existence of mobile phones on a very large scale, had been developed by the Brazilian anthropologist Darcy Ribeiro. For Ribeiro, the changes are not related to the existence or use of technology per se but the changes that occur in the process of dialogue between society and the world and between the various agents of society.[207] Indeed, the issue of communication is crucial at many levels because Latin American theologies are based on a communication between human beings and God within community rather than in virtual communities that control communication. The issue of access to communication does not have the all-embracing free access that the media portrays because the level of access to the internet depends on the provider and therefore on economic resources and services acquired and, at the same time, while it is true that the internet can be accessed through an internet café anywhere in the world, resources, financial resources and time, are also involved in this power struggle for faster and better electronic or wireless communication. If the daily task is to struggle for food, clean water and clothing, electronic communications are not part of a daily life of a globalized world but maybe the daily distraction of the gospel of prosperity or the gospel of emotional evasiveness. This point was clearly made by Patrick Claffey in his 2007 Africa Lecture at the University of St Andrews when he spoke about the fact that those who use the internet in Africa search for websites with products that they would like to acquire but they certainly do not have access to and will probably never have.[208]

In terms of daily social engagement, globalization has meant a more visible economic face so that 'the more visible process of globalization can be seen in the increasing interdependence of countries' economies and through the integration of markets, forming a single market'; however, for Leonardo Boff, 'this interdependence of countries' economies is, in fact, a dependence of peripheral countries on core countries, because the relations between countries are neither equal nor symmetrical, and without such relations there is no real interdependence'.[209] Those states at the periphery, as is the case with those human beings at the periphery, communicate within the locality and are given commands rather than dialogical communications from the centre. As issues of global warming have shown, however, the development of the centre affects the periphery and the comfortable lifestyle of a centre affects the periphery, be it in Europe, in Rio de Janeiro, Santiago or Buenos Aires.

The churches are used to processes of globalization and indeed Christianity can be held responsible for globalizing the planet through a direct involvement in colonial processes of the nineteenth century and the emphasis on Western education and trade supported by missionaries through the first part of the twentieth century in Africa and Asia. If at that time European powers were looking for trade and raw materials, throughout the twentieth century the United States became the central international and commercial power; as in the history of all empires, further and further economic and military expansion followed. Even Evangelicals, Mormons and Jehovah's Witnesses expanded within a connection between empire, Christianity and neocolonialism in Latin America. Today, the model of globalization creates barriers for the periphery and makes life poorer for the periphery to the effect that I would argue that such American globalization contradicts completely the biblical values of the Kingdom of God, the possibility of a socio-Christian utopia as interpreted by the social doctrine of the Church, and brings into question the credibility of Christianity within Latin America.

Within this chapter I explore three contemporary issues that clash with gospel values and Latin American theology: war, migration and global warming. They exemplify the challenges posed by the centre to the periphery and the historical misrepresentation of the values of the Kingdom within a society that considers itself Christian and the central player on the world stage, the US government, that over the years has led a crusade against extremism, non-Western values and any dissent over policies. The interesting fact is that the war on terror is focused on the periphery. All these global realities illustrate the deep contradictions between the preaching and life of Jesus of Nazareth and the appropriation and implementation of Christianity without spirituality, of prayer without conversion and of neocolonial power without liberation.

Theologies of War and Terror

The sad events of 9/11 and the terrorist attack on New York and Washington, DC, triggered the usual response: further attacks, further violence and further terror. War seems to be a human constant; statistics tells us that 'of the 3,400 years of human history that we can document, 3,166 have been of wars. The remaining 234 years were certainly not years of peace, they were years of preparation for wars.'[210] However, the conditions that followed 9/11 were a new development within war, so far understood as a war between nations such as the two world wars or between two neighbouring states. The so-called 'war on terror' created the conditions of a clash between the United States and its allies and the terrorists, for the most part Islamic fundamentalists. The phenomenon of terrorism is not new – most of the colonial powers experienced attacks by groups who wanted them out of their territories; however, the contemporary conditions of a globalized terrorism created a new phenomenon, a globalized war.

Within that globalized war, the United States and its allies fight against those who want to destroy Western civilization and Western values and, because those extremists are Muslims, there is an understanding of a clash of religions, Islam and Christianity. This is the point that in my opinion needs to be challenged. Neither Christianity nor Islam has in their scriptural foundations the possibility of raging war. Wars such as the Crusades or the War on Terror are political creations; those interpreting conflict and violence in the name of religion or of religious presuppositions are certainly manipulating the sacred and should not do that. The reality is that those political leaders, political commentators and analysts of security and terrorism understand the power of religion in creating and fostering violence rather than peace. In the Western context, the lessons of Northern Ireland tell us that the violent conflict was not religiously motivated but it was a sad conflict between social groups, their inclusion and exclusion within a contemporary state and the possibilities and impossibilities of achieving anything by violent means.

Let me state my position very clearly here. The only way of achieving peace in society is to provide the conditions for social justice and the only way of preventing the spread of terrorism is dialogue between nations, faiths and enemies. Violence and war are not conducive to such goals and only punish those who are the recipients of violence and suffering: the poor and the marginalized, the civilians caught in the lines of fire, the refugees, the widows and orphans of any military conflict. Already John XXIII had spoken in 1963 about the dangers and futility of war, and since then most of the Catholic bishops of the world, including those in Latin America, have condemned the use of force for just or unjust means.[211] Regarding the proliferation of weapons and the stocking of them, John XXIII was very clear, including the banning of all nuclear weapons when he wrote:

Hence justice, right reason, and the recognition of man's dignity cry out insistently for a cessation to the arms race. The stock-piles of armaments which have been built up in various countries must be reduced all round and simultaneously by the parties concerned. Nuclear weapons must be banned. A general agreement must be reached on a suitable disarmament program, with an effective system of mutual control.[212]

The advent of nuclear weapons and their proliferation within the so-called Cold War made it impossible to apply the principles of the 'just war' as understood many years ago when armies marched with horses or on foot and it was possible to count the number of soldiers and ammunition that an army could have. The decision, for example, by the government of the United Kingdom to explore the replacement of the nuclear trident submarines in 2007 was a disappointing reminder that even when all religious leaders followed the theological stand of John XXIII they were not heard by the leaders of a nation that takes part in a war on terror and remains a close ally of the United States.

The war on terror and the campaigns of 'liberation' by the United States-led coalition in Iraq in 2003 had implications for Latin America and for the poor and the marginalized of one of the smallest and poorest countries of the Americas, El Salvador. On 17 May 2007 Mgr Ricardo Urioste, former secretary and Vicar General of Oscar Romero, spoke at the Jesuit Spirituality Centre in Edinburgh as part of his series of lectures in the United Kingdom sponsored by the Romero Trust, a trust set up in memory of assassinated Archbishop Oscar Romero. When asked about the situation of the poor in El Salvador, he reminded his audience that soldiers from El Salvador had joined the US-led coalition present in Iraq and that the government of El Salvador, the only Latin American government that sent troops to Iraq, had to pay for their keep and their equipment. In summary, the government of El Salvador could not say 'no' to President Bush because they were dependent on US aid and military training as they had been 25 years before when the United States was pouring one million dollars a day in military aid into El Salvador in order to control the rebel forces.[213] Military tactics used by the United States in El Salvador in the 1980s were considered as ways of controlling insurgency in Iraq: thus the possibility of an 'El Salvador option' was discussed in 2005, whereby the US would arm some groups within Iraq so that they could control other undesirable groups. The US Ambassador to Iraq at that time was John Negroponte, who had worked in Central America under the Reagan administration.[214]

The Salvadorian troops arrived in Iraq in August 2003 and since then 5 army personnel have been killed and 24 injured.[215] The latest contingents to serve in Iraq were members of the Cuscatlán battalion made up of 379 soldiers.[216] The Catholic Church argued that Salvadorian troops should not be involved in somebody else's conflict and provided a united front with the Lutheran Bishop of El Salvador, Medardo Gómez, who interpreted the presence of Salvadorian troops in Iraq as a 'pact of fidelity' between the Salvadorian government and the US administration and condemned the use of the troops in this way.[217] Over the years, the Lutheran Bishop campaigned for the withdrawal of Salvadorian troops from Iraq.[218] Other public figures such as the Procurator Fiscal for Human Rights, Beatrice de Carrillo, argued that if at the start of the mission in Iraq it had had the backing of the United Nations the situation had changed dramatically and, following the example of the Spanish government, the Salvadorian troops should leave Iraq.[219] Other politicians who challenged the passive involvement of El Salvador's president Francisco Flores followed that position.[220] Despite the force of public opinion that wanted the Salvadorian troops out of Iraq, the Bush administration influenced the decision to keep them serving in Iraq by reminding the government of El Salvador that the US could interrupt the flow of dollars sent by Salvadorian families residing in the US that amounted in 2004 to 2,200 million dollars, equivalent to 48 per cent of all the Salvadorian foreign income.[221]

Theologizing this reality brings to mind the power and authority of the centre of gravity after 9/11 on the one hand and the use of the Salvadorian army to control and disarm another periphery, that of Iraq, on the other. Army battalions who slaughtered hundreds of Salvadorians after their training at the School of the Americas remain part of a bargaining power by the Salvadorian army. The descendants of the army personnel who killed the Jesuit community at the University of Central America become victims of the insurgency in Iraq, when they are killed or injured, while they are oppressors and perpetrators of an armed occupation in another country. Sobrino's classi-fication of 'crucified victims' applies not only to the families of the soldiers but also to those who suffer the Western powers' occupation of Iraq. There is only hope that one day the military battalions would be disbanded because they are still part of a war machine that does not fit within the values of the Kingdom. The budget for the Iraq operation by the Salvadorian army is spent on arms and military equipment rather than health or education for the people of one of the poorest countries in Latin America. Thus, a theologian cannot be convinced that any war on terror can be related to a Christianity outlined by the ministry of Jesus and his preaching about the Kingdom of God; further, a theologian cannot be happy about the oppression of a country that has suffered much, as exercised by its former colonial masters.

The Migration of the Victims

It is the machine of war, thirsty for blood and victims, that has provided one of the central theological tragedies so far not addressed by Latin American theology: migration and the social production of refugees. The first generation of Latin American theologians worked mainly on structural prophetism while the second generation challenged some of those assumptions by outlining the perspective of outsiders vis-à-vis the ecclesial community. The challenge of migration remains unexplored by Latin American theologians because it crosses boundaries and indeed globalized boundaries between the Americas. It is with the issue of migration that it would be possible to construct a contextual model of a theology of the Americas as proposed by Iván Petrella. The migration by the poor takes place from the rural peripheries of Latin America to other Latin American urban peripheries making the urban centres places of peripheral existence for many who dream of liberation from poverty, exclusion or persecution. The movement to the urban centres provides anonymity and a new start but in only a few cases provides all that had been dreamt before. Even when in the urban centres there are more opportunities there is also a divide between urbanites and country people, between those who hold the key to employment and opportunities, usually established urbanites, and those considered newcomers. The migration out of the urban centres also occurs and the landscapes of well-to-do families living outside the cities has multiplied in response to increasing urban violence and the return to a colonial aspiration to own land, to have family space as well as the latest four-wheel drive vehicle and a nice swimming pool. In the theological assessment by José Comblin:

> The ruling classes have chosen to flee, going off to live away from the cities, and that trend can only spread. The problem is for those who remain behind, and for the church that remains behind or sets itself up in the midst of violence.[222]

Theologically, the Gospels address the issue of refugees and migrants within the narrative of the departure of the Holy Family towards Egypt caused by the possibility of persecution by King Herod (Matthew 2.13–15). Within the magisterial teaching of the Church there has been a renewed sense of a changing world in which boundaries and territories are not sufficient for the interrelation of peoples throughout the world. Thus, John Paul II expanded on migrants and refugees in the following terms:

> More numerous are the citizens of mission countries and followers of non-Christian religions who settle in other nations for reasons of study or work, or are forced to do so because of the political or economic situation in their native lands. The presence of these brothers and sisters in traditionally Christian countries is a challenge for the ecclesial communi-

ties, and a stimulus to hospitality, dialogue, service, sharing, witness and direct proclamation.[223]

The reality of migration was also discussed by the Latin American bishops at Santo Domingo in 1992 as an expression of the negative individual and collective phenomena of contemporary Latin America.[224] The ecclesial stress on migration relates to the possibility that immigrants into the urban centres become less active in the Church and lose track of their socio-religious roots. Indeed, that is a relevant preoccupation. However, apart from the Jesuits' concern for migration at a level of a globalized Latin America,[225] there is the need to think of migration in terms of a theological centre–periphery axis of peace and liberation. In the case of North America and the immigration of thousands of Latin American later reclassified as Hispanic and Latinos there is a religious and theological contribution coming out of the globalized periphery.

The migrant is not 'a problem' but a human being with talents, with dreams, a son or daughter of God entrusted with the beauty of being and with the beauty of recreating the earth, entrusted by God through work. The border division between Mexico and the United States, for example, emphasizes the division between the white and the indigenous, between the North and the South, between Protestant and Catholic, between American and Hispanic, between worlds that remain perceived as colonizer/colonized, white/indigenous, civilized/uncivilized, godly/ungodly, etc. Despite the danger, thousands of Mexicans attempt the crossing knowing that if they are caught they would lose and if they are not caught they could die of hunger, thirst and heat exhaustion. Despite those dangers, Mexican farmers such as Juan Flores, a 31-year-old, attempt to get some help in their poverty. Flores 'talked about the needs of his wife, and of their dreams for their three children, especially his newest son, born just two weeks earlier. He said he was determined to try. "Of course I am scared", Mr Flores said. "But it's better to be scared and try to make a better life for my family than to stay and watch them go hungry".'[226]

During the 1980s and 1990s, the United States had re-enforced border patrols in order to prevent more immigrants from Latin America entering the USA illegally by crossing through the Mexican borders. However, in 2006, President George W. Bush requested the construction of a longer and more secure wall extending through 1,200 kilometres between the USA and Mexico in order to prevent more illegal immigration. The bill was connected with the possibility that terrorists could use this way of access into the USA. For once, President Vicente Fox complained of an American lack of vision owing to the fact that for Fox, and despite the large wall, Mexico would still remain a single nation, made of those inside the Mexican national territory and those outside.[227] The European Union Ambassador in Mexico and Austrian Ambassador Werner Drummel also condemned the building of the wall and requested from the Mexican president new initiatives for economic progress within Mexico so that fewer Mexicans would have to leave their own country.[228] The combined body of USA and Mexican Catholic bishops also expressed their concern about the development of a new wall that intended to divide families further and that de facto created a symbolic association between immigrants and migrants in general and criminals.[229] The Mexican House of Deputies also condemned the plans by the USA administration requesting that the Mexican president file a diplomatic protest against the USA administration because aspects of the new law regarding immigration to the USA not only related to the building of the wall but also linked illegal immigrants with possible acts of terrorism and curtailed the rights of thousands of Mexican illegal immigrants who had been living for years within the United States.[230]

The borderland wall extended by the USA government provides a physical and symbolic barrier that remains a migrant nightmare because it divides the possibility of a positive sense of globalization. Hispanic and Latino theologies have addressed the social realities of those Latin American immigrants to the United States while liberation theologies have addressed the poverty and oppression of those who live south of the USA wall.

Both theologies have failed to address the in-between because the in-between is volatile and peripheral to Latin America and to the United States. However, it remains a central landscape for the action of God who still loves the migrant and the one who is trying to enter the United States. Are there narratives about God among those who are preparing to attempt the crossing of the Arizona desert? How do they speak about God in their economic oppression and depravation? Are there dreams of grace, liberation and redemption among them? Are there parallels between the passage from Egypt to the Promised Land in the narratives of Mexicans who with a bottle of water and a few tortillas attempt the crossing? Or is it more appropriate to relate their experiences to the exiles that were brought from Judah to Babylon?

I would go as far as to argue that the theological bridge between a theology of the Americas and a Latin American theology lies within the action of God and the narratives of those who are today waiting to cross outside the land borders between Zapata-land and Gringo-land, between the wall that separates the North from the South as the Berlin Wall separated the East from the West during the Cold War. On which side of the wall is God? Is he waiting on both sides or on one? Is God trying to cross the Arizona desert? Is God being crucified by the US patrols? On which side is heaven and on which side is hell? Are those crossing representing the contemporary People of God? Many questions and many narratives arise out of the Gringo Wall because the God of the poor and the marginalized is moving out of the lands of milk and honey of South America into other pastures, other deserts, other urban centres, other realities. The 'irruption of the poor' has arrived at the wall and those within the fortified city see only thousands of uncivilized and dirty peasants who would destroy the American dream of clean, beautiful and aesthetically agreeable bodies, landscapes and futures.

A Latin American theology of migration is linked with globalized aspects of the dehumanizing market in which human beings are not at the centre. A Latin American theology of liberation needs to engage itself with the borders, with the borders as peripheries and with the borders as peripheral locations of God and the victims. It is there that the crucified victims encounter God in passing, in journeys, in a pilgrimage across a wall and a desert that could end with their physical passing into another life, that of the eternal Kingdom rather than the life of an illegal worker within the United States. The possibilities for other theologies are there, theologies that confront the idols of the market by centring their discourses in the subject of the wall and in the relocation of those crossing as agents of life while the governments of Mexico and the United States remain entangled in economic cooperation at the globalized level, trafficking business people and economic advisors as agents of death and agents of the non-Kingdom and the non-human.

Actions by Christians and by theologians around the wall would be a clear testimony of the irruption of the poor and the solidarity across the wall, balloons of hope and dance when families are reunited and when the scandal of human separation stops and ends for ever, utopian actions that can rekindle the hermeneutics of suspicion about economic policies that need human beings as cheap labour and that discard them when they are no longer of use to the market.

The description by Ivone Gebara of the Peasant Women's Movement whose members invaded multinational laboratories in Rio de Janeiro in March 2006 are pertinent here because they represent the crucified who live in hope and who challenge a theology that cannot stand at the wall and with the God of the migrant and the marginalized immigrant:

> Eyes reddened from fatigue and suffering, eyes greyed by fear and the injustice of the present and the past, eyes green with hope from thinking of fields full of beans and maize and of smiles of children who are not hungry. And the mixture of colours in their eyes and their bodies turned into life-and-death actions necessary for supporting their own lives. This was a significant event for the great majority of rural women in Brazil: Does it pose any challenge to theology?[231]

Those civil movements of challenge and protest question the oversimplified view of the market because those who suffer, the victims and the crucified of Latin America, are telling public opinion a different story, not from their assumed passivity but as agents and actors in the ongoing building of the Kingdom of God.

Global Warming

If war and economic deprivation are central causes for migration throughout Latin America natural disasters seem to be occurring more and more. The planet in which we live is warming up. While initially there is an optimistic note because those of us in particular who live in colder climates would like to feel warmer part of the year scientists and development agencies are telling us that global warming provokes longer dry seasons and drought as well as extra rain and thus floods. Global warming 'is caused primarily by human-induced imbalances of carbon dioxide and other trace gases in the lower atmosphere'.[232] It is a situation where regardless of the globalized discussions on global warming by the centre it is the poor and the disadvantaged of this world who are suffering and are bound to suffer year after year.

Already the Latin American bishops in 1992 recognized that ecological issues related to the planet in general and to Latin America in particular were to become important for the churches and for theologians because of the slow destruction of the planet.[233] Latin America has the largest rain forest in the world and the Amazon region holds the key to future generations and their survival. How are we to theologize about ecological issues and global warming?

First, by recognizing the situation and second by returning to the sources of an ecological theology, a Latin American ecological theology that emphasizes people's stewardship of creation rather than individual private property of land, sea and air. Third, by taking once again a utopian political and Christian commitment to guard and restore what is God's by right and people's by adoption into God's family. For the situation is serious, as described by Leonardo Boff:

> The dominant patterns of production and consumption are causing environmental devastation, the depletion of resources, and a massive extinction of species. Communities are being undermined. The benefits of development are not shared equitably and the gap between rich and poor is widening. Injustice, poverty, ignorance, and violent conflict are widespread and the cause of great suffering. An unprecedented rise in human population has overburdened ecological and social systems. The foundations of global security are threatened. These trends are perilous – but not inevitable.[234]

Leonardo Boff has gone further in arguing that Christian theology over the centuries has been co-responsible for the ecological crisis. Indeed, the texts of creation that have defined the boundaries of a godly creation of human beings as centre to creation have been misinterpreted so that the first chapter of the book of Genesis, clearly a temple litany for liturgical purposes, indicates the possibility of a creator God who gives dominion over creation to human beings but does not give ownership to them. In the second chapter of the book of Genesis and within another account of God's creative activity human beings are moulded and fashioned from the earth, lovingly, in order to remain united with the rest of God's creation and not to overload creation; once again the aspect of stewardship and the passing of time is marked by the fact that once Adam and Eve had trespassed the rules of engagement given by God they were not welcomed within the garden any longer. They had to leave.[235]

The implications of such a short liberating exegesis connect human beings with the universe through a refreshed understanding: human beings were created to remain in communion with the universe – the universe was not created for humanity. Human beings as stewards of planet Earth have failed to protect the structure of the planet, a fact that has triggered the growth of an eco-politics that continues to inspire human communities. Latin American theologians have supported the eco-political movements because it is in those protests against the destruction of the planet that the discourse about God and the discourse about human beings and their rights have encountered each other. Indeed, Leonardo Boff has linked eco-politics and ecological liberation with the option for the poor, the majority of people, so that 'the challenge will be to bring human beings to realize that they are a large earthly family together with other species and to discover their way back to the community of the other living beings, the community of the planet and the cosmos'.[236] Others, such as Ingemar Hedström, have reinterpreted that option for the poor as 'an option for life' so that 'to exercise this option is to defend and promote the fundamental right to life of *all* creatures on earth'.[237]

As outlined in other chapters, the reality of the North and the South of planet Earth is very different because the current ecological crisis comes out of an overuse of resources, the greed of multinational companies and the impossibility of cutting gas emissions because of the politician's need to please voters in the United States. Nevertheless, there is an emerging unity between theologies of the North and the South that relate to these ecological issues. A globalized ecological crisis has made ecological theologies a global phenomenon because it affects not only the poor of the Third World but also all the citizens of Europe and North America. Discussions on private property, national property and the globalized/universal property of the Amazonian forest have created a momentum for theological discussions that bring together concerns for a way of life and a way of ownership with an ethical edge at a worldwide level.

For, if Sallie McFague can imagine 'the world to be God's body', then, by our actions, we are in connection with an incarnated God who 'becomes dependent through being bodily in a way that a totally invisible, distant God would never be'.[238] Christian action precedes theology once again and the act of theologizing comes closer to a social and political act in which experience and the experience of God's body, that is, the planet, become crucial to understanding our need of God and our need to see her in creation, a practice very much linked to the indigenous cosmologies of Latin America upheld by the *pueblos originarios*, the stewards of creation before the arrival of Europeans in the Americas, the stewards of creation before the arrival of Christianity in Latin America.

What to do about the global phenomena of war, forced migration and global warming? We must provide a Christian response through social activism as a way and means of theologizing, of encountering God and his work on this planet. In the words of Seán McDonagh, 'Since global warming has the potential to cause massive pain to human beings and destruction to the earth, every individual and institution should do what they can to halt it.'[239] Latin American theological methodologies have already provided a link between social action, theology and God at the local level. Less has been directly said, however, about involvement with larger political movements in a globalized Latin American context. This is the subject of my theological explorations in the next chapter.

8

Political Activism

The globalized contexts in which Latin American theologians argue for a hermeneutics of suspicion have had a constancy of purpose: religious commitment to praxis, that is to the paradigms of the Kingdom that in turn made them challenge unjust social structures. If at the time of the military regimes all religious activism became political it is possible to argue that the realm of the religious and the political cannot be separated because, as the world created by God is one, so is society in Latin America: there is a unity between the religious and the political, and theological reflections do not reflect a separation between religion and politics but a reflection on the political. Every human act is political because it expresses an intention, a belief or a being through a body, and the body is present within the corporeality and the physicality of a landscape, a group, a society, a ritual system and a particular location.

Liberation theology as a phenomenon was disliked by traditional Christians because, according to them, liberation theology politicized religion, that is politicized pious devotion and articulated piety within a social and a cultural context. Maybe it was for some, particularly in North America, the wrong politics for the wrong piety. Nevertheless, it coincided with an emergent social and political phenomenon, that of political activism. If Christians and guerrilla movements encountered each other it was not because they had the same political ideas but that they had the need and possibility of challenging the status quo, one group with arms, the other with the message of the gospel. Figures such as Thomas Merton or Daniel Berrigan in the United States inspired a generation of Christians to challenge the impossibility of peace and the impossibility of social change. They redefined the possibility of a passive resistance by changing it into an active Christian witness to other values, other lives and other utopias. This chapter explores the possibilities and limitations of Christian political activism and a theology of political activism from the point of view of the poor and the marginalized, a much-needed response to contemporary social problems such as the inequality of ownership of land, the destitution and marginalization of indigenous groups and the oppression of women, trafficked children, and the victims of economic structural adjustment, globalization in general and a free market economy in particular.

Activism and Politics

After the period of the military governments and the return to democratically elected governments throughout Latin America there was a shift in activism and Christian activism. Previously all efforts by civil society were geared to avoid further violence and there was a general denunciation of a systematic process of human rights violations. In democracy, the shift took place from a very public and politicized role by the Christian communities to a less prominently public but nonetheless effective one through NGOs, educational projects and civil organizations addressing problems of land or indigenous disputes. The 'enemy' of a Christian vision of equality was not the State any longer but the face of private international corporations that had been given significant authority, financial and legal, by the military regimes. Human beings became less important than the market and a less powerful State devolved part of its role to private contractors, thus reducing state spending on social welfare, health and education.[240]

The involvement in politics by Catholic priests, condemned by the Vatican, during the period of the military regimes was changed by a further involvement of Christians in party politics and within more globalized organizations such as Amnesty

153

International. Organizations such as Amnesty challenged the democratic states' inability to cope with deep changes in a social structural model that was geared towards economic success and less to the equality in law of all citizens. The election of several socialist-oriented heads of state in Bolivia, Brazil, Chile and Venezuela pointed not to a return to old models of politics but to a popular concern for change and state involvement rather than the ongoing support for highly privatized financial states unable to speak by themselves within the international community. Popular movements of protest arose in Argentina and Bolivia, challenging the State and providing new avenues for a Latin American theologizing.

The Latin American bishops in Santo Domingo had already in 1992 emphasized the involvement of lay Catholics within politics, stressing the importance of the social doctrine of the Church, the involvement of Catholics within the daily running of a world created by God and the possibility of changing some social structures that were sinful and didn't reflect the values preached by Jesus in the Gospels.[241] These lay ministries, according to the Latin American bishops, derive from the incorporation of all the baptized into the Church and from the commitment to discipleship and witness taken through the sacrament of Confirmation.[242] Once again it is worth mentioning here that within Latin American politics there has been a long history of Catholic involvement in politics. In the case of the Evangelicals or the Pentecostals there are varied responses to the same social realities and certainly politics are distinguished from religion, looked at with suspicion and with some detachment. The reasons for this approach to politics are varied; however, one of the central theological understandings is that 'Spirit and Word tend to be rather loosely related to the church because the latter is conceived as a voluntary association'.[243] Within that complexity of ecclesial responses, Miroslav Volf has managed to restructure this somewhat free and loose ecclesiology by replacing the Catholic role of the bishop as the centre of unity with that of the laity as a theological body of believers.[244]

Latin American theologians have taken part in a social and public witness to change in society, using the practice of Christian pilgrimage with song, prayer and chant as means of protest, of awareness and of community activity. It is within the *caminata* (the walk), a public procession from a church community to a local centre, to another parish, to a central government building, to a privatized piece of land, to a police station or to a military base that theologians experience and listen to the narratives about oppression/liberation, life/death, justice/injustice, violence/peace and sin/grace. The physical single journey becomes a metaphor of the Kingdom where people united by faith and by a need to journey together to the Kingdom chant, talk, exchange views, make friends, share jokes, share food and arrive united and strong at a point of sociopolitical conflict.

Through the *caminata* or *marcha* the people of God take over, temporarily, the public roads and the public spaces and make their voice heard on behalf of the whole community. It is through the passing of the people of God that political authorities are alerted to their needs and their voice on behalf of the poor and the marginalized. It is a fact that it would be quicker to arrive in buses or cars to the intended destination but it is through the *caminata* that Christians share their lives, their hopes and sometimes their anger. It is through the *caminata* that a bodily commitment to theology is made because it is the body rather than the pen that challenges the unjust status quo of Latin American society.

In September 2006 I had the opportunity to attend the academic event that marked the centenary of the birth of the late Chilean Cardinal Raúl Silva Henríquez in Santiago, Chile. The day coincided with a general strike and protests by secondary school students requesting free tickets for public transport and more say in the ongoing discussions of educational reforms in Chile. As thousands of students entered the city centre the police contingency grew, armed for war, wearing body armour unseen even in Britain and similar to that worn by soldiers in Northern Ireland or while on duty in Iraq. Reports by Amnesty International condemned the use of force against the students and some of the bystanders had to run, as they had when younger, from the rubber bullets, the tear gas and the general confusion. I remember walking with the President of the Cardinal's Foundation and a Chilean bishop trying to talk to the police who wanted all to be arrested regardless of their age. Among the youth groups marching with their banners there were members of the Christian communities supporting the right to free education in Chilean society. The event included lunch for bishops, invited theologians like me and the lady Minister of Education. It was a very pleasant and delicious lunch during which the minister faced more questioning from the older protestors than from the youth. There was no doubt in anybody's mind that theologians and staff members of a Catholic University were together in the *caminata* with all the students. That was a political act as well as a Kingdom act.

For every political act in which the values of the Kingdom are upheld there is a Kingdom act that opposes a passive endorsement of the status quo. Therefore in Christian political activism the emphasis is on the social construction of meaning as well as the possibility and the urgency to influence policy. It is not a choice for those baptized but it is one of the responsibilities arising out of baptism. Those baptized in Christ share in his life, and his life as portrayed in the Gospels was one of deep communion with his Father and intense communion with the lives of the sick, the dispossessed, the oppressed and the poor of his time in general. The experience of social solidarity and a shared humanity becomes then an experience of God and a realization of the Kingdom to come, here and not yet.

The contemporary realities of politics in Latin America suggest that there is a disinterest in politics as a result of the very high expectations that were created after the period of the military regimes and the fact that political power has not been given back for the most part to the voters and to the people in general. Others suffered the trauma of the military regimes and needed time to themselves so that José Comblin has convincingly argued that:

Many have left politics to take refuge in their own selves. They have discovered their psychological problems and their personal needs. They have gone on to believe that political involvement has caused them to waste time, and they are striving to make up for that lost time. Military regimes left their imprint on many people who have no more energy for plunging into conflicts again. They want peace and contentment.[245]

As a result of that change towards being inward-looking individuals, they searched for values outside the Christian communities and they enjoyed their awakening as self-motivated actors within globalization. The economic elites and the media aided that change with dreams related to material goods and the ongoing exposure to television channels more interested in virtual television than in political discussions of substance and about governmental policies. Within those changes the Christian activists became fewer in number but changed their involvement with major political parties to involvement with NGOs and localized organizations that were working in projects rather than social change. There is a limitation in the changes that Christian activists as theologians can generate within the Church; however, if we are aware of that limitation we can move to the further possibilities within a periphery–centre utopia. This is the terrain where liberation theology as 'a theme park', as a fashionable product to be purchased, in the words of Marcella Althaus-Reid, tends to disappear or evolves into the complexities of a Christian utopia.[246]

Activism and Utopia

The act of theologizing at the periphery suggests by its mere location that the act of doing theology is a political act that challenges the injustice and centrality of the State and develops through a committed action with others a symbolic meaning, a political meaning and a Kingdom meaning. In doing so, the political activist comes closer to God because he or she openly proclaims the centrality of God as just, as active, as present in the periphery and, as a result, challenges the centre. The utopian actualization of the memorial of Christ's death and resurrection takes place in the Eucharistic celebration and in the political act, within the private–public, within the Church–periphery association. The combination of the two realms of meaning creation allows for an inclusion of the periphery, not a full alliance of those excluded from the Church and those excluded from the periphery. Both meaning-makers together allow for a challenge to the centre because the centre as monolithic sensor cannot react well to the challenges by the excluded as well as by those who connect with the periphery, and indeed are part of the ongoing making of the periphery within any nation state.

The Christian utopia is radically dislocated when a theological act becomes fully political and fully subversive and allows the actor, the activist, the gay and the priest to challenge any unified subversion. Within that activist horizon of ethical indignation 'a vision leads one to see the prevailing situation as ethically unacceptable, that is, as a situation that must be transformed'.[247] As a result of such indignation the hermeneutical circle understood as a circle of meaning is always difficult to figure out when the creation of meanings cannot be controlled but remains autonomous, changeable and unclassifiable. This is the Christian utopia per se: the aesthetic expression of a God who cannot be contained within any human taxonomy and who allows further explorations into the utopia of the human and the divine together. Althaus-Reid expresses these possibilities in terms of the end of 'entertainment' due to the fact that 'the constructed utopia of liberation is not, in the real world, the coherent narrative that theology wants'; for Althaus-Reid 'Christianity is a utopia, and the actual process of utopia-making is basically diasporic, made of identity shifts at different levels but basically at the level of differentiating desires'.[248]

The difference between a 'theme park theology' and a theology at the periphery is the level of altruism that the activist at the margins is able to provide. Altruism is understood here as the possibility of giving one's life for others in a utopian manner, hoping that an altruistic act, word or thought would help others. Jesus' death on the cross becomes an altruistic political act because without going into a high theology of atonement and other academic discussions Jesus of Nazareth gave his life for what he believed and didn't run away from the possibility of dying for his friends, that is, for those he had embraced and welcomed, mostly those rejected by the society of his time. I would argue that Christian altruism as discipleship of a victim and a crucified, Jesus of Nazareth, is located within the periphery and that it is the periphery that attracts people from the centre in a linear circle periphery–centre–periphery and action–reflection–political action–altruistic solidarity–Kingdom of God = theologizing. Thus, the process of theologizing starts at the periphery and returns to a peripheral location, that of the Kingdom of God as anti-poem, anti-market and anti-value. Theologizing becomes political activism because it has started from a social action in solidarity that has led to a further emptying of the self and of the self's content. The altruistic process of peripheral solidarity then can have three circular and co-related processes fulfilling the characteristics of the both/and context of community and individual:

1. Altruistic solidarity with the self
   Due to contextual circumstances an individual or a community becomes involved in a process of cooperation, of solidarity with others within a much localized periphery.
2. Altruistic solidarity with a group
   The actions and reflections of that particular group within the periphery builds up a Christian anger towards an unjust situation and a common theologizing takes place whereby avenues of hope and utopian understandings of the Kingdom of God take place. As a result the group decides to have a *caminata*, to journey towards the centre of power in order to challenge the status quo.
3. Altruistic solidarity with those unknown
   The actions and reflections from the periphery, already

expressed at the centre create an altruism of solidarity with other peoples, other marginalized and other peoples even when those people's problems are not the problems of the group or individuals in category (1). Risks and political activities related to the Christian values of the Kingdom of God are taken in order to help others rather than ourselves; these actions differentiate altruistic attitudes and actions from organizational and structural empowering.

4. Altruistic solidarity from the centre towards the periphery
   The periphery remains the centre of political activism and religious solidarity; however, members of the centre join the periphery not because they suffer the same problems but because they yearn for an altruistic life based on the values of the Kingdom of God.

The difference between charity and theologizing lies within the nature of the action: one aims at helping the marginalized in their need, the other helps in the same way but also questions the structural conditions that have created the social condition of a marginalized. Even when at the level occupied by the media and the literary critics it seems that contemporary Latin America is dormant when it comes to Christian altruism. This is indeed the situation created by the media, always dominated and owned by the economic elites and their agendas. It is impossible to believe that any theologizing at the periphery is not taking place; the reality is that the world outside Latin America is not receiving information about those processes of theologizing, while my own students, living for short periods in Latin America, report back enough examples of the agency of the poor in the periphery, which suggests that the media is interested in the global phenomena rather than in what is happening at the grassroots of Latin American social movements. For example, there are very few works on the theologizing on torture and the actions/theologies produced by a group of Christians in Chile in the 1970s under an umbrella group known as the Sebastián Acevedo Movement against Torture (*Movimiento contra la tortura Sebastián Acevedo*); however, it is possible to argue that, as well as the Madres de la Plaza de Mayo movement in Argentina, there were extended discussions on those issues following from actions of protest and searches by thousands of members of the Christian communities all over Latin America.[249]

In assessing processes of altruistic theologizing it is necessary to move diachronically because the action of a group of protestors against torture had its roots in the actions and reflections of a group of committed Christians twenty years before the actual public appearance of the Sebastián Acevedo group. The group Equipo Misión Obrera (EMO) was a group of committed Christians, worker priests, nuns and laypeople who in the 1970s gathered together information about social problems in order to support their members' work for human rights, community life and the values of the Kingdom of God as lived by Jesus of Nazareth in the Gospels. After the 1973 Chilean military coup the group became involved in sheltering and helping the persecuted by the regime and supporting initiatives that would help restore civic rights in Chile. The group did not condemn violence in itself but pledged not to use it themselves. In 1983 and within the climate of generalized public protests against the military regime, torture became systematic not just in secret detention centres and as implemented by Pinochet's secret police but also as common practice throughout police stations, where tools for torture were kept and where torture with electricity was systematically used.[250] Along with the atrocities already experienced by Chileans under the military regime, that practice made matters worse and the group asked themselves what they should and could do in those circumstances.

One of the main characteristics of the social process of torturing is the silence and complicity by torturers, those tortured and their families, the media and those who hear about it. When people were arrested and tortured, others would say that such activities were not without reason: thus those arrested became suspects. The group decided that a public denunciation of torture as an inhuman form of interrogation was needed. The group was inspired by the Ghandian philosophy of non-violence and anybody taking part in the actions of the group was expected not to exercise any violence against the police or the torturers. The movement against torture accepted members of other groups that advocated violence, for example, the Movimiento de Izquierda Revolucionario (MIR), but within the group there was no room for any violence. The first public action took place on 14 September 1983 in front of the barracks of the political police (CNI) at Borgoño Avenue in Santiago. Five steps were always followed with military precision: (1) a banner was hanged at the front gate of the police station; (2) a short public address alerted those passers-by that within those walls the police were torturing citizens; (3) the group sang a song; (4) the group stopped the traffic; and (5) they waited for the police to arrest a few participants as they could not arrest them all. Friendly media was invited to record the protest and friends of the movement took part as spectators. A Jesuit, Fr José Aldunate, became the spokesman of the movement and it grew into a large movement of altruistic support for the victims of torture. The initial action in September 1983 had already gathered 70 people. Between September 1983 and the start of 1990 the group took part in 80 public protests in front of police stations and became well known within Chilean society.[251]

What made the group an altruistic group from the periphery confronting the centre? First of all, there was a deep spirituality of solidarity with others framed within the life of Jesus of Nazareth and his relevance for the world. Second, there was a Durkheimean 'organic solidarity' in which the support for others in return meant the support for oneself, and third, there was a deep sense of anger about the victimization and ill-treatment of human beings, an anger that was channelled into peaceful protests rather than into further violence. That 'organic solidarity' made the group cohesive, determined and fearless. If Christ and Sebastián Acevedo had given up their lives for others there was no way in which we could avoid supporting others in their actions to save human beings from barbaric attitudes that opposed completely the values of the Kingdom. Was it an extreme resource within an extreme period of history? Yes. However, it was not very different in motivation from the contemporary actions by the Peasant Women's Movement in Brazil who, on 8 March 2006, entered the laboratories of the multinational processing plant of Aracruz in Rio de Janeiro in order to uproot the genetically modified eucalyptus. In the explanation given by Ivone Gebara, these were 'violent but tender actions, contradictory actions, full of love and justice, full of hatred of injustice. Never mind interpretations; what matters is to accept that this happened and to try to understand it.'[252]

Who was Sebastián Acevedo? This is the hermeneutical question that allows understanding of a theology of individual narratives, probably as important as the 'irruption of the poor' as a pointer to further theologizing, and not fully developed within contemporary Latin American theology. I never met him and he probably never met most of the people involved in the movement that took his name as a banner of hope and a challenge to the centre and to torture centres as extensions of that centre. On 11 November 1983, two months after the foundation of the movement against torture, Sebastián Acevedo, a 50-year-old worker, burned himself to death in front of the Cathedral of Concepción. Acevedo, father of María Candelaria and Galo Fernando, two youngsters who had been arrested by and remained prisoners of the security services, had exhausted all legal appeals to have them returned by the police while he knew that they were being tortured.[253] He paid the ultimate price as a protestor against the regime and against the systematic use of torture for political means and ends. The movement against torture adopted his name as a sign of an immediate need to stop suffering, torture and violence in Chile, and in any case there was no choice – many endured the police water canons and the gas canisters.

Activists for Peace

The methodology adopted by the movement against torture is helpful as a methodology of liberation and as a school of theology. The group had to ask questions about social practices of death and about a culture of death in general. All of them decided to act publicly in order to bring into being social conditions for life and for hope in the future. Their reflection on the consequences came after their action, knowing that the majority of the Chilean population knew that torture was being used but very few decided to do anything about it.

The contemporary signs of death in Latin America are slightly different. Indigenous activists in Chile are still arrested and die under suspicious circumstances in police stations in southern Chile. However, the death of human beings due to financial policies and the lack of social welfare in the Latin American states fulfil the conditions where actions for liberation and for peace precede the popular theologizing of a Kingdom that was supposed to arrive with the return to democracies in Latin America but never did. Has God gone asleep in contemporary Latin America? I do not think so. The God of Life is still requesting the followers of Christ that they watch for the signs of oppression and death and side with the poor and the marginalized in their struggle. The temptation is different, and in Nancy Cardoso's assessment: 'Living in Latin America means always and again living the conflict and confrontation of not letting oneself be seduced by the wrong choices of the Empire, which take us far from what we love and from our liberation struggles.'[254]

The choices are personal as well as community oriented and the choices can lead to death by avoiding Christian activism and the challenges of theologizing as well as death by challenges to unjust structures and those who create them. In February 2005, for example, Sister Dorothy Stang, an American Sister of Notre Dame de Namur, was walking to a meeting of poor farmers at the small village of Boa Esperança, near the town of Anapú, in the Amazon region of Brazil, when two men approached her and pointed their rifles at her. She took her Bible from her shoulder bag and read aloud, 'Blessed are the peacemakers for they shall be called the children of God.' She was shot six times at point blank range and died beside the road. Sr Dorothy had arrived in Brazil in 1966 and had been supporting poor farmers who had been given small plots of land expropriated from the big Brazilian landowners; she had even campaigned for federal land to be made into a safe reserve for poor farmers.[255] Her case is not isolated because every Christian activist for justice and therefore for peace is at risk of being attacked and silenced by those involved in drug trafficking, children trafficking, women trafficking, extortion, fraud and corruption and illegal appropriation of indigenous lands for profit through sales to multinational companies.

Those who campaign for justice and therefore prepare society for a life in peace believe in the utopia of the Kingdom of God and their theologizing takes place even at the periphery of the State. For the State sometimes does not understand the possibility of a clear stand regarding the implementation of peace by rejecting any kind of violence on anybody but particularly on the poor and the marginalized. The liberation of those altruistic agents of the Kingdom requires in the first place that they identify themselves completely with the attitudes and the liberating choices of Jesus of Nazareth within the Gospels.

Among the characteristics and daily movements of the Spirit expected from them and from all those involved in processes of theologizing for liberation are the following: prophetic indignation, compassion in solidarity, ongoing activity to cut free from every type of mooring (whether physical or spiritual, social or religious), promulgation of putting the poor first, in this world, on the way to the reign of God, constant communion with others, filial communion with God the Father, and family sharing with all, but above all with the poor, the outcasts, the non-citizens, the non-persons, the outlawed, those who 'subvert' the various established (dis)orders.[256] Further, they are expected to maintain a utopian attitude stating with their lives that 'a different world is possible', even when through a process of 'utopian ingenuousness' (a term developed by Franz Hinkelammert) those who are satisfied with the world as it is have convinced all others that such a utopia is 'a society that produces no more utopias'.[257]

Peace is the objective of a Kingdom-oriented activism at the periphery, a peace that signifies the arrival of the Kingdom in which children and the vulnerable can laugh and eat plenty and in which all kinds of violence and injustice have been excluded from the ordinary life of all, not of a few elites with more than they need while the majority of the poor struggle to feed themselves. That peace of theologizing at the periphery does not require a theoretical contradiction between public/private. The challenges to the centre, thus the public contestation of a non-utopian society, comes out of an ordinary life within the periphery in which the ethical and the aesthetic are complementary and not in collision. Thus, Gustavo Gutiérrez through his life in the periphery has probably gained more authority to speak than the usual eco-activists or eco-terrorists; for Gutiérrez asserts that 'Only if we know how to be silent and involve ourselves in the suffering of the poor will we be able to speak out of their hope.'[258]

One of the great anti-values and scandals within the globalized community but particularly within the Latin American context is the enormous expenditure on arms and weapons rather than on social services. The justification for those weapons is that they would be valuable tools that would reduce conflict and violence either as deterrents or as much-needed instruments to guard peace. The periphery rejects such a statement and all Christian activists for the Kingdom should do the same. Isolated examples are organizations such as the Fellowship of Reconciliation, Greenpeace or anti-nuclear weapons activists present in Latin America; moreover, political analysts have acknowledged that there is a growing sector of NGOs supporting further democratic rights and democratic institutions in an emerging democratic Latin America.[259] However, Latin American theologians have always rejected the possibility of controlling violence with more violent actions or weapons of destruction. Dom Helder Cámara, the Brazilian archbishop, spoke in the 1970s about the cycles of violence that start with one violent action and escalate through further cycles of violence in response to violence.[260] Peace in Latin America will not exist until all weapons and all armies are dismantled and when just structures do exist within the State and within the churches.

In a thoughtful argument José María Vigil has contrasted the God of War with the God of Peace. Within that comparison the male structural and hierarchical God of War gives authority to injustice and conflict while the God of Peace provides the possibility of dialogue and the common good at the centre of society. Thus, Vigil argues that 'The God of war . . . demands human sacrifices: someone has to accept the harsh side of reality; someone has to be at the bottom; someone has to die so that we can live, prosper, develop. It is "natural" and inevitable that there should be losers, people left in the margins, excluded'.[261]

The contrasting vision of the biblical text embraces beauty and divine energy for those who follow its lead into the heart of the prophetic message of peace and prosperity associated with justice and the presence of God in religious practices placed at the centre of human society, as an expression of the belief that war is not needed and that the God of War was left behind in a distant past of men who wanted to assert their own identity and their own selfishness through war. Thus, the biblical vision speaks by itself: 'He will wield authority over many peoples and arbitrate for mighty nations; they will hammer their swords into ploughshares, their spears into sickles. Nation will not lift sword against nation, there will be no more training for war' (Micah 4.3 [JB]).

The values of the Kingdom cannot be compromised but they are clearly binding for all Christians who seriously believe in a Kingdom that is above the State and above all petty differences, sectarianism and social exclusion. Since the 1960s just war theorists and pacifists have been portrayed as within opposed camps so that, because of the complexity of the invasion of Iraq and other international military interventions, Lisa Sowle Cahill has even suggested that 'peacemaking and reconciliation are aims which ought to unite just war theorists and pacifists in a new era when the dangers, excesses, and inevitable injustices of war are clearly seen by all'.[262] I am afraid that I consider that position too optimistic and I am not a pacifist per se; however, without condemning the just war theory, it is possible to argue that when there are nuclear weapons, long-range missiles and the latest infrared technology to attack and destroy it is impossible to judge the possibility of the just measure of force to be used in combat. I remember that when in May 2005 I hosted the former commander of the British desert rats regiment of the 1990 Iraqi campaign, Major General Patrick Cordingley, for a lecture, he clearly indicated to me that ethical considerations of volume or force didn't come into consideration when it came to making sure that men under his command were equipped to win a battle and not to be killed; he needed more tanks and more armed power than his enemy in order to advance and therefore protect his men from getting killed. The nuclear question is one that consumed already two generations of ethical discussions without dwelling on the fact that any use of force relates to the failure of the secular systems of political government and international relations when it comes to securing peace in all regions of the world.

Ernesto Cardenal has probably been the only Latin American theologian of aesthetics who managed, because of his period as a novice of the Trappists in the United States, to rescue the Christian urgency of building peace from within, through acquiring the attitudes of the contemplative who dwells on the love of God and neighbour in order to assess sociopolitical situations in the light of the attitudes of Jesus of Nazareth. The influence of Thomas Merton and the discussions that took place almost forty years ago at the time of writing are relevant to a liberationist theology of peace, particularly at a time when there is a proliferation of nuclear weapons and Latin American governments have not embraced disarmament and peace as their democratic agenda. On the contrary, the economic violence on the poor continues while a part of the military budget of the rich nations would manage to cover, for example, free primary education for all children of the Third World.[263]

Merton in a letter to Ernesto Cardenal wrote the following hopeful but controversial note, a note that, written more than forty years ago, still resounds as the reality for Christian activists today:

I say the future belongs to South America: and I believe it. It will belong to North America too, but only on one condition: that the United States becomes able to learn from South and Latin America and listen to the voice that has long been ignored (a voice which even ignores itself and which must awaken to its own significance), which is a voice of the Andes and of the Amazon (not the voice of the cities, which alone is heard, and is comparatively raucous and false). There is much to be done and much to pray for.[264]

These are the themes of the following and last chapter, the future of a theology that has diversified itself but that is and will remain fully grounded on the context of the poor and the marginalized of society rather than on a set of philosophical presuppositions that impede the possibility of embracing the dreams and utopia of what sometimes can only be understood as the 'irrationality' of God and of his Kingdom.

9

Theological Advocacy and the Periphery

As previously argued the developments of theology in Latin America since the 1960s have been unexpected, surprising and exhilarating.[265] If one were to assess the continuities between such theological movements and the grassroots of Latin American Christianity it would be possible to return to the discussion generated by Juan Luis Segundo and related to the kind of liberation theologies that emerged or certainly the possibility of complementarity between 'two kinds of theology', an academic and a popular theologizing.[266] In my opinion, there is room for both kinds of theology not only within the 'theme parks' production of theology criticized by Marcella Althaus-Reid but also within the wide spectrum of hermeneutical suspicions held by those inside the churches, those outside the churches and those firmly based within the alternative centrality of the Latin American periphery.[267]

The strength of Latin American theology is manifold but two traits remain central for ongoing developments: it is a grounded/contextual theology and it is a theology that maintains a preferential option or a single option for the poor and the marginalized.[268] However, within those general epistemological considerations and within an ongoing epistemological continuity of Latin American theology for the twenty-first century there are some themes that will become rather important within ongoing changing contexts of injustice and oppression within and without the Church.[269] In this final chapter I would like to outline them in order to summarize my own epistemological markers for future developments. They are idiosyncratic markers in that all contextual theology is a contested field of interpretation; they are personal in that my own journey with God has brought me to the realities of the poor, sometimes against my own will. Now as part of the theological production of liberation theology I find myself wanting to outline them as sources of personal challenges as a Latin American, as an exile and as a migrant who has lived in several places in the world over the years. With Gutiérrez I can finally argue that 'It is for us to find our own route amid the present sufferings and hopes of the poor of Latin America, to analyze its course with the requisite historical effectiveness, and, above all, to compare it anew with the word of God.'[270]

The Context of the Theologian

One of the presuppositions of European theology has been that there is a universal canonical way of doing theology, the correct one always centred upon philosophical presuppositions. Even as a student I remember being taught the different subjects that constituted theology and the tools of theological thinking through the Christian Scriptures and as a Roman Catholic through the centrality of the *magisterium*/tradition. That has been somehow changed by the ecumenical development of localized theologies and by the enormous amount of work in non-European theology as well as by the efforts to understand interfaith dialogue and the relation of Christian theology with world religions that have taken place since the 1960s. However, within Latin American theology there has been too much emphasis on abstract categories such as 'the poor', 'the people', the Basic Christian Communities and even 'the Church'. The use of Marxism as a hermeneutical tool created a set of epistemologies that sometimes operated in the same abstract way as European theology but managed to be grounded within the social and ecclesial experience of those who were theologizing.

Nevertheless, in most of the Latin American theological writings there was a complete absence of self-reflexivity; some would say that this is a good sign. I would argue that sometimes Latin American theologians have been misunderstood by readers because they have not developed a narrative regarding the actual context in which they wrote something, thus leaving their ideas in an abstract context. For example, at the beginning of his work on Job, Gustavo Gutiérrez explains the context in which he developed his ideas in a very abstract manner, stating that part of it was related to 'the Latin American experience', and further warning the reader that 'Explicit references to it will not be many; nonetheless this experience – and its present-day variations – are in a sense the source that points to a set of problems, raises questions, and guides the discussion'.[271] The writings of, say, Elsa Tamez, Marcella Althaus-Reid and Frei Betto, among others, have corrected some of this abstraction by starting their own theologizing and their writing with some of the social and personal narratives they have witnessed and that have triggered their thoughts about God, the Church and the poor.[272] Althaus-Reid, for example, writes: 'I was an adolescent when my family faced eviction. We were given 24 hours to pay overdue rents or leave our house. When the police arrived my mother and myself moved out our few belongings on to the street: some bags of clothes, a box with tea and rice, two chairs.'[273] More of this self-reflexive and personal style could be used within the actual construction of a written Latin American theology.

In volumes I and II of *The History and Politics of Latin American Theology* I tried to ask more contextual questions about the actual life, likes and dislikes of theologians from the first and second generation because I felt that I could not understand Gutiérrez or Dussel without knowing more about them. Much more of this approach is needed, a biographical or auto-biographical living statement that connects with the narratives read by those who are interested in the theological works coming out of Latin America.[274] This more self-reflexive style of theological writing would not only clarify some of the mis-understanding about Latin American theology but it would also avoid the danger of creating yet again canonical works of an idealistic type rather than ongoing theological discussions on changing realities concerning a God who changes and surprises us with her presence in our own *caminata*.

I find myself amused by the fact that within a whole range of Latin American theology my personal experience of a journey with God of almost fifty years doesn't allow me to disengage context from theology, God and Church from theology. Here there is a concrete limitation in every theologian; however, there is still the possibility that the diversity lies not in a common agreement but in a different experience and understanding of the same divine, human or theological reality. Thus, the forthcoming theological reflections by such as Iván Petrella, Marcella Althaus-Reid or me have something in common: we have all been cultural products of the Southern Cone and we have all been hybridized by living, working and studying somewhere else. Three of us live outside our countries of origin as migrant workers, immigrants into the systems that we ourselves challenge through theologizing. However, our hybridism has a unique difference: we have a different understanding and experience of gender, relations with the churches, faith or agnosticism, and dislocation/migration. Those differences remain possible to think but difficult to tell. Moreover, within those experiential differences the theologies of the poor stand as the primary focus and genesis of our own narratives but the differences in the genesis of experience create a final text that is somehow different even when possible, plausible and certainly challenging for those outside the peripheries of the world.

Is it possible to construct theological texts without understanding the genesis and fibre of a person? I don't think so – there is no theology without experience and there is no academic theology in writing without understanding the genesis of the theologian. The process of initial immersion of a theologian as part of a community is what makes theologizing possible and not the other way around. I would not be a theologian if I had not had two periods of intense experience within two very different contexts. I have mentioned my 'forced immersion' in a

Santiago shantytown from 1977 to 1979 in which I learned more about hermeneutics than I could have through a class in a university. Let me rephrase this. I would not have understood half of what I later studied in a university in Europe without having taken part in the community discussions about the gospel that took place within Christian communities at difficult political and religious times in Chile. At that time and within a frontal clash between the Church and the military, theology was not a systematic subject but a way of life, and theological discussions on the Church, on ministry, on hermeneutics and practical theology took place in all small Christian communities. To be a member of one of those communities was to transgress the established order which had proclaimed an orderly God who had blessed the military with the mission to regain Christianity as part of Christian civilization from the threat of the 'Marxist cancer'.[275]

The image of God and my experience of the divine changed from that of a pious ritualistic master of the universe to a friend, to a crucified, to a living pilgrim who loved us because most of the well-to-do and the beautiful people would not have been in El Pinar during the protests or would not have been involved in reflections among congregations which had policemen and informants present as well as those tortured, the persecuted and the members of groups that advocated violence. It would take a whole monograph to narrate how much fear I had in those years, how much adrenaline my body produced but how much I came to love the Church and the Jesus of the Gospels. That is why I remain with Gutiérrez and others not fully satisfied by some of the Catholic Church's policies but at home in the celebration of the sacraments and a daily routine of reflection and prayer even after all these years.

Theologizing outside the Church

It is possible to argue that the process of theologizing is not a doctrinal manoeuvring of available elements as in the case of a casuistic argument of logical possibility/impossibility. Instead, it is a hermeneutical process of interpretation out of action with suspicion of whatever is already theologized. What is God doing and saying in a particular context and a particular situation is the relevant question. There are writings, councils and structural passages that help us develop some interpretations by challenging others' interpretations, but certainly faith without understanding would not be conducive to an experiential theologizing within Latin American Christian communities. The Latin American case has been a clear example of particular emphases on context and a contextual God whose theological understanding was not developed before but that cannot be constrained by a particular understanding. As there are many Christian traditions it is not possible to say that there is a unique theology, a unique methodology or a unique belief within the whole realm of theologies arising out of the many contexts in which Christians, Muslims, Buddhists or Jews are involved. I am always aware that to become a Muslim the neophyte needs to make a simple profession of faith asserting the oneness of God and the centrality of Mohammed as God's prophet, a simple theological statement that brings that person into the Muslim community. In asserting that theological statement, a person is making a choice and asserting a personal belief; within a larger world of theologizing that statement is one within many others, at least within societies that accept principles of religious pluralism.[276] Thus, I have been somewhat sceptical of a unique theological centrality of the Christ event as outlined by Evangelical Christians; I prefer the concept of a *caminata* – a history of salvation in which God has been present among many peoples and many events in the history of the world. Thus, my position vis-à-vis the world religions is that of those who advocate *inclusivism* rather than *exclusivism*, people such as Paul Knitter. I am a Roman Catholic but I cannot exclude the possibility that God has plans of life/salvation for others; I am a creature and as a theologian I do not have access to all God's plans for the present or the future.

This brings me to my certainty that theology as action and

theology as academic discipline can take place outside the canons and traditions of the Church and that it can be interpreted as a narrative by those with faith, without faith or even with another faith. I repeat, my personal vocation is of a theologian with faith and seeking understanding through a daily practice of the Roman Catholic tradition; however, I must locate my own journey within a place outside Latin America as well and an encounter with other believers, those honest, devout and God-fearing people outside the Christian tradition. Between the years 1987 and 1990 I lived and worked in Kenya, and within the years 1987 and 1988 I was part of a team of Roman Catholics living among Muslims in north-eastern Kenya, in an arid and isolated bit of Kenyan desert, in a small village called Garba Tulla, with a nomadic population of around 5,000 people of which less than 1,000 lived in town at any given point. This was a sobering process of theologizing and my memories of sitting outside the house in the heat of the evening talking to somebody who was not a Christian emphasized my delight at being there with God and also my delight to discover that the same God could work within different languages, traditions and peoples of the world.[277] Within the harshness of life of the desert, conversations about God followed actions of support for others as nothing could be done without the help of many; at the same time there was no need to philosophize about God's existence as everybody, Muslims, Methodists, Roman Catholics and Mennonites, believed in God despite the fact that Allah had an overwhelming number of followers praying five times a day while the small Christian group kept to morning and evening prayer only.[278]

Theologizing outside the Canon

After that experience I decided to acquire some tools from the social sciences because there were many aspects of my own experience of God and my life in Kenya that needed explaining. Of course, I had returned to Nairobi in 1988 and for two years

I was part of a team of Roman Catholics living in the slums of Nairobi supporting biblical and prayer groups. The social outreach of those groups was amazing and a truly unique theology of liberation arose out of their action within the slums and their evening reflections on the biblical text. Parting was hard because the small Christian communities of the Nairobi slums were very similar to those in Latin America and I was returning to London and the life of a student again and to the Latin American community of exiles in the big city.

However, the cross-fertilization of those experiences of Latin America and Africa remained for several years in my writings and I returned to Latin American research in 1999 when I visited the Villa Grimaldi, a previously wonderfully beautiful Italian villa on the hills of Santiago that after the military coup was used as a torture camp for systematic interrogation and for the worst instances of torture in Chile during that period.[279] It was William Cavanaugh who linked in a symbolic interpretive way the practice of torture with the Eucharist, and I found myself asking questions about what had happened in Latin American theology in the previous years.[280] Thus, my previous volumes reflect my answers to those questions.

It is clear from these investigations that there are several interesting aspects of a socioreligious reality in Latin America that still need to be explored; of course the advantage of having a theology based on experience and context is that the context is always changing and theologies are always evolving as far as human beings do not part from the centrality of the poor in God's plan and do not fall into the trap of a 'utopian ingenuousness' (a term developed by Franz Hinkelammert).[281] The ethical realism of a *caminata* beckons and the pilgrims do not cease to journey but stop whenever new markers of God's presence are found along the road: the presence of the marginalized, the suffering pilgrims and the dispossessed either by the world or by the churches.

It is also clear that the development of a Latin American theology for the twenty-first century cannot be a programmatic or systematic way of doing theology but must respond to social realities in which theological praxis and hermeneutical suspicion are to be applied in order to respond to God's call and his Kingdom. It is here where the two theologies outlined by Juan Luis Segundo would have to co-exist, even when not talking to each other. The themes that I will consider next are theological investigations that respond to contemporary realities of oppression and injustice in Latin America and that, as an academic theologian, I can decide to explore in my next academic work. However, those theological explorations can only exist if there has been a contextual understanding and a real social action that triggered their mere possibility of existence.

Theological Advocacy

There are parallel realms of theologizing as Diego Irarrázaval could be dealing with a *caminata* in Santiago as he works in a parish or Iván Petrella could be engaged in dialogue with Latinos or Afro-Americans in Florida. I read, write and share theological explorations coming out of my yearly incursions into oppressed worlds, but like Juan Luis Segundo my daily engagement is with groups of students, exiles or political activists who need further information about injustice in Latin America and further challenges in their own European *caminata*. Theological advocacy emerges here as a theologizing outside the theological canon because the writing of theology becomes a cry on behalf of the poor and the oppressed in order to awaken further ruptures in the deadly embrace of the consumerist and selfish US empire, a shock to the globalized tentacles of the beast of hedonism, selfishness and discrimination.

These ideas could be a product of my own weekly work on behalf of asylum seekers and their lawyers' search for experts on their countries of origin who can testify at the courts or through a written legal statement that the refugees' stories match the knowledge of a person who is considered an 'expert' on that country, region, political process or recent violent episode. For example, the courts tell a refugee from Rwanda that he is lying because it could not have been political persecution after the Rwandese Patriotic Front of Paul Kagame took over the country and the 1994 Rwanda genocide ended. My role is to match the refugee's legal statement with the historical facts and, in most cases and to the annoyance of the authorities, they match. Thus, my ongoing theologizing comes out of a daily encounter with narratives of political violence, rape, abuse, trafficking, slavery – which in turn create refugees living in fear, rejection, oppression and injustice. All these people are in need of liberation and they represent the face of Jesus in our European milieu. However, they also represent the voices of the oppressed Third World that challenge their theologians back in Latin America, Africa and Asia and they challenge us. My students usually make the remark, as most of my teaching is full of gruesome details of violent and concrete suffering: 'another one of his happy subjects!'

Indeed, the life of a theologian who has been raised in the Third World is a difficult, challenging and sometimes exhausting life but a happy one. I lived through the so-called 'golden period' of Christianity in Chile, treasured what Muslims taught me about God in Kenya, planted trees with Latin American refugees in Scotland, marched with workers and peasants in the midst of tear gas and the batons of the police, cried for loved ones in previously known torture camps, and now I have the chance to keep learning from the rising ecological movements, women's movements and peasant organizations in Latin America as well as from the realities of refugees in my country of adoption. There is a mediatory theological bridge that arises out of those involved in praxis and those who are writing academic theology, led always by those involved in theological praxis but necessarily allied to those who can in the name of the Kingdom of God exercise a certain theological advocacy for the poor and the oppressed of this world, so that their voices are heard and their oppression ends on their own terms and according to their own wishes. Within that theologizing there is the ethical immediacy of advocacy because no theology is neutral, out of a particular or non-canonical context in some way.

Further, it is important to realize that human beings as refugees and as 'victims' have been located at the centre of God's contemporary acts of salvation and grace. Thus, Jon Sobrino's interpretation of Ignacio Ellacuría's theology has pointed to the fact that 'these "victims of today" bring salvation, which also means salvation in history. Israel's servant has been used in classical soteriology, but the historical salvation brought by the servant is a product not of the world of abundance but of the Third World.'[282]

Within the expansion of Latin American theologies, within the expansion of those theologies of the 'victims', there are other areas that have remained more unexplored and certainly outside the canons of historical European theology. I would like to mention two areas of theologizing as possibilities for further investigations within Latin American theologies of the twenty-first century.

Aesthetic Theologizing

Ernesto Cardenal recalls in his memoirs a piece of graffiti in the Nicaraguan city of León that carried the following message: 'El triunfo de la revolución es el triunfo de la poesía.'[283] 'Revolution's triumph is poetry's triumph' embraced the realities of all the Latin American struggles for justice and peace in which poetry and literature played a significant role. In that respect, Cardenal's accomplished life as a poet was not an exception to the life of Latin American students who in following revolutionary causes nourished their personal love for a loved one or their love for social processes of change with reading and writing of poetry. Campaigns for literacy meant that Latin American peasants were empowered with human dignity by being able to read and write; even before those campaigns took place, however, the strength of a Latin American oral tradition meant that poems were memorized, recited and shared around campfires, ecclesial communities and during a *caminata*. The central texts used by those reciting morning and evening prayer within the Latin American Church were the psalms, the cultic poetry of Israel, and Leonardo Boff in his recent work has returned to the beauty and consolation of the psalms by suggesting that 'The Psalter has always served as a book of consolation and a source of meaning, especially when humanity is battered by helplessness, persecution, injustice, and threat of death.'[284]

Within a continent with several Nobel Prize winners of literature and with accomplished poets, even revolutionary ones such as Pablo Neruda, it surprises me that there has not been the development of a Latin American theology of aesthetics, of beauty, not a systematic examination of God's attributes, but those attributes as understood by communities in action, communities who wrote poetry, painted, composed songs and developed theatre. Maybe the 'preferential option for the poor' and the close association of the arts with the middle classes prevented this; nevertheless, from the Mexican muralists to Neruda to the Cuban revolution social processes of change have been filled with new arts of hope, change and utopia. The poets among Latin American theologians, such as Ernesto Cardenal and Pedro Casaldáliga, led the way; others must follow, for the liberation by God is present in the liberation of free spirits who can express themselves in hope and trust and who after oppression compose canticles of freedom, of joy and of love. Love and utopia come together in a theological reflection on the action of love, the action of sharing and the actions of solidarity with the poor and the marginalized. New aesthetic expressions in Latin American theology could include paintings, poetry and drama in which, by sharing the utopia together, liberationists and theologians could share the possibility of adding beauty to the struggle, beauty to the eruption of the poor and beauty within the periphery. For example, in the peripheries of the large city of Santiago, outside walls of apartments are regularly painted with scenes of life and with graffiti of hope; buses and trucks are painted with messages of liberation; poetry is read by those who survived Pinochet's persecution; and the victims bring beauty and hope to the rest of society.

Thus, inspired by that communal experience of communal Wednesdays of poetry with survivors of torture and liberation struggles, I wrote on the occasion of the restoration of a series of rosebushes in March 2007 at the infamous torture camp of Villa Grimaldi on the hills of Santiago:

Humanidad hedionda y carcomida
Humanidad sangrienta y vomitada
Sentías su presencia y su amargura.

Sentados en la oscuridad empañada
De los ojos salientes de locura
Se olía un aroma divino,
Un aroma de plata y de medusa.[285]

Worm-eaten and stinking humanity
Bloody and vomited humanity
You felt her presence and her sadness.

Sitting in the soiled darkness
Out of the sunken maddened eyes
They smelled a divine fragrance
A scent of silver and of Medusa.

The prisoners of the Villa Grimaldi smelled that scent, that fragrance of the roses, while sitting on a bench, blindfolded, feeling the cold of the winter and the warmth of the summer. Underneath that blindfold they felt the immediate liberation of the spirit while aspiring to a physical liberation from prison. Those who were at the margins of the gospel dreamt of a voice from the Vicariate of Solidarity that would help bring them back to their loved ones. They didn't fear death but they feared life without utopia, without a dream, without the possibility of a better world. They didn't fear torture but they feared life in a world without beauty, without poetry, without warmth and love, even when their love was mechanized by the possibility of being caught and never to be with them again. In one case, that of Alvaro Miguel Barrios Duque, arrested in August 1974, it is possible to suggest that a number of members of the Movimiento de Izquierda Revolucionario (MIR), a paramilitary organization targeted by the Chilean military after the military coup, read and were influenced by the American poet Walt Whitman (1819–92).[286] Whitman worked tending the wounded in the Washington hospitals during the American Civil War, and through his poetry and his journalism he expressed his witness to suffering and his scepticism towards the US government policies of his time.[287] The Chilean poet Pablo Neruda not only included Whitman in his section of the *Canto General* 'Que despierte el leñador' but also dedicated an ode to Whitman.[288] Whitman's poem 'O Captain! My Captain!', considered as a song of glory and death, could have been used by Alvaro Barrios as a reflection of his own time. The last line of the poem reads, 'walk the deck my Captain lies, fallen cold and dead'.

The theologizing of beauty and struggle, of oppression and literary freedom seems to be missing from the possibility of theologizing option and struggle, liberation and utopia within the Kingdom of God in the context of the sociopolitical contexts of the 'golden age of Christianity in Latin America'.

Theologizing Peace and the Periphery

Another area that is still to be developed within Latin American theology relates to the theology of non-violence, non-violence understood as the action by Christians and others against the given narrative of war and the possibility of the existence of any armed conflict that finds authority in God. I speak here about challenges to the possibility of an imperial army trying to solve violence in Iraq by means of force as well as Muslim fundamentalism trying to kill in order to show allegiance to God. Within the Latin American context, however, there is a conditioned nationalism with certain militarism that needs to be challenged by the God of Peace and the actions of his followers.

Most of the history of Latin American nations is taught at

schools and is understood throughout one's life by following
the history and usually the defeats of national armies. In Chile,
for example, a national holiday takes place on 21 May, a date
that commemorates the sinking of a Chilean navy vessel, the
Esmeralda, in the context of the 1879 Pacific War between
Chile, Peru and Bolivia. As a child, I went to the Mapocho rail-
way station in Santiago where navy personnel arrived from
their headquarters in Valparaíso in order to take part in military commemorations in Santiago. Their crisp and clean
uniforms inspired several of my school classmates to join the
Chilean navy and we met years later in public spaces when they
were trying to clean Chile of the 'Marxist cancer' and I was trying to protest against the use of torture by my dear classmates.
I must admit that Chilean education is so engrained in me that I
still feel drawn to watch military troops in wonderfully colour-
ful uniforms on parade. Deep down though I know that behind
the military uniforms the State has made human beings into
killing machines; however, in the case of Latin America there
has not been much theologizing done about a God that sup-
ports different armies who kill each other in the battlefields.
The transition from the military to the civilian governments
made it impossible to challenge the possibility of large South
American armies being still in place but some protests against
the Chilean symbol of the brave navy, the vessel *Esmeralda*,
which was used to torture citizens and to transport Marxists,
have already been seen in Valparaíso and throughout the world.
Does the Christian population of Chile still believe in the God
of War? Are they aware of the possibility that the poor and the
marginalized could have better social services if the armed
forces were to be cut to a minimum size and budget? Is the God
of War and the formation of killing machines compatible with
the message of the Beatitudes (Sermon on the Mount) or
the practice of Christianity in Latin America? Here I refer to the
address by the Jesuit John Dear to the 2005 meeting of the
International Thomas Merton Society when he said:

The wisdom of non-violence teaches that: War is not the will of God. War is never justified. War is never blessed by God. War is not endorsed by any religion. War is the very definition of mortal sin. War is demonic, evil, anti-human, anti-life, anti-God, anti-Christ. For Christians, war is not the way to follow Jesus.[289]

There is also a close relation between military conscription and the poor because those conscripted usually come from poorer backgrounds by reason of the fact that those who have an educational or financial future are not conscripted into the army. Is it not the time that peace and the periphery work together by theologizing against the use of God for military purposes and of the Christian message for authorizing the increasing of wars and conflicts as well as for the use of illicit methods of terrorist prevention, such as 'rendition flights' or interrogation with torture on prisoners without legal defence, such as those in Guantánamo Bay? I would argue that in a globalized world and a globalized context, all Latin American nations are part of a trend that has created more conflict and war in the name of international security for peace. In the Gospels, it is justice that creates peace not force or the accumulation of security reports or weapons of any kind.

The Development of Theologies

The both/and paradigm which I used at the start of this work defines social action as a mediatory outcome between action/reflection, between the individual and the community. If one returns to the initial paradigms and dicta of liberation theology one realizes that difficult conflicts and complex contexts provided the possibility of a firm and active theologizing, with theology as 'a second act'. The reading of hundreds of works by Latin American theologians has left me with the same sense that I have on the restorations of faith and doctrine proposed by Benedict XVI: it is not preservation or restoration that is at stake when it comes to the churches or a particular kind of theology. The values of the Kingdom as exemplified by the life of Jesus of Nazareth, and the Beatitudes, remain central for theologizing. Thus, my sense is that there is always a future for Latin Americans theologizing through actions in response to, in particular, new contexts. A theological life that looks *ad extra* and not *ad intra* refreshes reforms and informs the journey of a people towards a better world here and now and a newer promise in the afterlife. The *caminata* continues anew and there are signs that the best is still to come. We don't yet know how it will look but it will come out of the people of God journeying together in hope; it will come not out of the learned but from the victims, those who bring salvation to a world in need of justice and peace. It will come out of the periphery rather than out of the centre and it will certainly not come out of further elaborations of economic policies from above or from new understandings of methodological tools spoken and used by the centre.[290] This is the utopia of the Kingdom, bruised but never beaten completely, sad but never hopeless, angry but never violent, walking but always with suspicion, interpretive but always singing, citizens but always alien, misunderstood but never alone. It is from the experience of the poor and the marginalized that Latin American theology arose; it is from them, their contexts and aspirations that further theologies will come out – but that is another story.

Notes

Introduction

1 Mario Aguilar, *The History and Politics of Latin American Theology*, Volume I, London: SCM Press, 2007; Volume II, London: SCM Press, 2008.

2 See Juan José Tamayo, 'Reception of the Theology of Liberation', in Ignacio Ellacuría and Jon Sobrino (eds), *Mysterium liberationis: Fundamental Concepts of Liberation Theology*, Maryknoll, NY: Orbis; and Blackburn, Victoria: CollinsDove, 1993, pp. 33–56.

3 The position of John Paul II vis-à-vis communism was understandable as the Catholic Church in Poland had to deal with communist-imposed regimes, and, as remarked by the historian Eric Hobsbawm 'In some countries of "real socialism", as for instance Poland, it was possible to avoid the Party in one's dealings with colleagues and friends' (Eric Hobsbawm, *Interesting Times: A Twentieth-Century Life*, London: Abacus, 2003, p. 147). For an assessment of John Paul II's influence on the perception of a unified Europe, see Patrick Michel, 'John Paul II, Poland and Europe', in Alberto Melloni and Janet Martin Soskice (eds), *Rethinking Europe (Concilium* 2004/2), London: SCM Press, pp. 124–8.

4 For a fuller study of 'the people of God' within the Bible and the Christian tradition, see Juan Antonio Estrada, 'People of God', in Ellacuría and Sobrino (eds), *Mysterium liberationis*, pp. 604–14.

5 At the theological level African and Latin American theologians encountered each other through the Ecumenical Association of Third World Theologians (EATWOT) and the first period of their work was coordinated by Enrique Dussel and François Houtart; see a useful historical overview in Enrique Dussel, 'Theologies of the "Periphery" and the "Centre": Encounter or Confrontation?', in Claude Geffré, Gustavo Gutiérrez and Virgil Elizondo (eds), *Different Theologies, Common Responsibility, Babel or Pentecost? (Concilium* 171, 1984/1), Edinburgh: T&T Clark, pp. 87–97. See also EATWOT, *The Emergent Gospel*, Maryknoll, NY: Orbis Books, 1976. For a theological overview, see Theo Witvliet, *A Place in the Sun: An Introduction to Liberation*

Theology in the Third World, London: SCM Press, 1985. An Asian Christianity, a Christian project, was more problematic. Numbers of Christians in Asia, with the exception of the Philippines, remain small and the post-Vatican II discussions on salvation within the world religions created more than an impasse between those who adhered to a Christ-centric option (exclusivists) and those who understood the world religions as places where God could save (inclusivists): see Paul F. Knitter, *No Other Name? A Critical Survey of Christian Attitudes Towards the World Religions*, London: SCM Press, 1985.

6 In taking the Marxist concept of praxis, the theologian of liberation sided with Marx's response to philosophical ideas, particularly those of Feuerbach, and Marx's criticism that those ideas didn't change anything. Thus, for Marx, there is a need to make an option first, that of changing society, before thinking about ideal worlds. Therefore the sense of an orthodoxy as the right praise or the correct doctrine is replaced in liberation theology by the right option for the poor before theologizing any Christian doctrine in a particular context; on Marx and praxis vis-à-vis theology, see Gregory Baum, 'The Impact of Marxist Ideas on Christian Theology', in Gregory Baum (ed.), *The Twentieth Century: A Theological Overview*, Maryknoll, NY: Orbis; Ottawa: Novalis and London: Geoffrey Chapman, 1999, pp. 173–85, at p. 182.

7 The appointment of my classmate and friend Carlos Pellegrín Barrera SVD as bishop of Chillán in southern Chile during 2006 is an example of this policy. Bishop Pellegrín studied theology in Europe with an emphasis on the study of the missiological sciences and served as a dedicated missionary in Ghana, West Africa. On his return to Chile, he worked supporting lay missionary groups and was elected rector of the Colegio del Verbo Divino in Santiago, where I studied myself, serving in a very conservative milieu that made him into a very conservative person. I have no doubt that Bishop Pellegrín would serve as a very dedicated and pastoral bishop – he is indeed a very pastoral and friendly priest – but I doubt that the diocese of Chillán would be pushing for any groundbreaking theological and pastoral model that would depart from administering the sacraments within a pastoral model of good relations with the civil authorities and those who own the land within Chillán. Chillán will follow pastoral policies that could be implemented in any other Catholic diocese in the world without looking at issues of justice and peace or the centrality of the margins within a much-needed reconciliation in truth and a new agrarian reform. I would hope that the future proves me wrong in my current assessment.

8 Baum, 'Impact of Marxist Ideas on Christian Theology', pp. 182–3.

9 See Aguilar, *History and Politics of Latin American Theology*,

Volume II, and in particular Marcella Althaus-Reid, *From Feminist Theology to Indecent Theology*, London: SCM Press, 2004, and Iván Petrella, *The Future of Liberation Theology: An Argument and Manifesto*, Aldershot and Burlington, VT: Ashgate, 2004; later edition London: SCM Press, 2006.

10 Sometimes it is difficult to distinguish political theology and a theology of the political within theology as an academic discipline. I can only say that if political theology asks questions about the possibility of applying Christian canons and given paradigms within the running of a state, a theology of the political perceives God and the Church as part of society, not apart, and therefore asks questions about the role, mission and social immersion of the churches within the following given paradigms: all religious acts are political and the churches are to immerse themselves in all realms of life because God has been immersed in the world of human beings since the creation of the world. For practical purposes political theology remains a European endeavour while a theology of the political has been part of the involvement of the churches and Christian theologians within the Third World. For an excellent treatment of the ideas at stake within European political philosophy and theology, see Raymond Plant, *Politics, Theology and History*, Cambridge: Cambridge University Press, 2001.

11 Marcella Althaus-Reid, 'The Divine Exodus of God: Involuntarily Marginalized, Taking an Option for the Margins, or Truly Marginal?', in Werner Jeanrond and Christoph Theobald (eds), *God: Experience and Mystery* (*Concilium* 2001/1), London: SCM Press, pp. 27–33, at p. 33.

12 Willem Frijhoff, 'Church History without God or without Faith?', in Erik Borgman and Felix Wilfred (eds), *Theology in a World of Specialization* (*Concilium* 2006/2), London: SCM Press, pp. 65–75, at p. 72.

13 Nigel Rapport, 'The "Contrarieties" of Israel: An Essay on the Cognitive Importance and the Creative Promise of Both/And', *Journal of the Royal Anthropological Institute* 3, 1997, pp. 653–72.

14 Aguilar, *History and Politics of Latin American Theology*, Volume I.

15 Aguilar, *History and Politics of Latin American Theology*, Volume II.

16 On Gutiérrez, see Aguilar, *History and Politics of Latin American Theology*, Volume I, pp. 21–40; and on Casaldáliga, see Aguilar, *History and Politics of Latin American Theology*, Volume II, pp. 135–49.

17 Petrella, *Future of Liberation Theology*, p. 146.

18 Marcella Althaus-Reid, *Indecent Theology: Theological Perversions in Sex, Gender and Politics*, London: Routledge, 2000, p. 200.

19 Rapport, '"Contrarieties" of Israel', pp. 653 and 654.

20 Althaus-Reid, 'Divine Exodus of God', p. 29.

21 The importance of the body in the history of political processes and historical developments within Latin America has been richly explored by the contributors to Lyman L. Johnson (ed.), *Body Politics: Death, Dismemberment, and Memory in Latin America*, Albuquerque, NM: University of New Mexico Press, 2004.

22 Jon Sobrino borrows this concept from Ignacio Ellacuría: see Jon Sobrino, 'Redeeming Globalization through Its Victims', in Jon Sobrino and Felix Wilfred (eds), *Globalization and Its Victims* (*Concilium* 2001/5), London: SCM Press, pp. 112–14.

23 See Pedro Casaldáliga, 'Open Letter to the Soul of Brazil', in José Oscar Beozzo and Luiz Carlos Susin (eds), *Brazil: People and Church[es]* (*Concilium* 2002/3), London: SCM Press, pp. 123–8.

24 Raul Julia and Richard Jordan, *Romero*, 1989, directed by John Duigan.

25 For the possibilities of ecclesiological models, see Avery Dulles SJ, *Models of the Church: A Critical Assessment of the Church in All Its Aspects*, Dublin: Gill & Macmillan, 1976.

26 *Lumen Gentium* § 9–17.

27 I refer to John Milbank, *Theology and Social Theory: Beyond Secular Reason*, Oxford: Basil Blackwell, 1990, chapter 8; for a good summary of Milbank's overreading of Marxism within liberation theology and his wrong assumption that all liberation theology comes out of the Catholic Church, see Nelson Maldonado-Torres, 'Liberation Theology and the Search for the Lost Paradigm: From Radical Orthodoxy to Radical Diversality', in Petrella (ed.), *Latin American Liberation Theology*, pp. 39–61.

28 *Corpse Bride*, directed by Tim Burton and Mike Johnson, 2005.

29 Gustavo Gutiérrez, 'Speaking about God', in Geffré, Gutiérrez and Elizondo (eds), *Different Theologies*, pp. 27–31, at p. 30.

30 Gutiérrez, 'Speaking about God', p. 31.

31 Jim Forest, 'Communities of Resistance', in Alistair Kee (ed.), *Seeds of Liberation: Spiritual Dimensions to Political Struggle*, London: SCM Press, 1973, pp. 29–36, at p. 29.

32 On sociability, God and the Trinity, see Christoph Theobald, '"God Is Relationship": Some Recent Approaches to the Mystery of the Trinity', in Jeanrond and Theobald (eds), *God*, pp. 45–57. Within Latin American theology the Trinity has been developed under the realms of community and social activity: see Leonardo Boff, 'Trinity', and José Comblin, 'The Holy Spirit', in Ellacuría and Sobrino (eds), *Mysterium liberationis*, pp. 389–404 and 462–82.

33 Examples of these individual narratives are found, for example, in

Notes

Adam Jones (ed.), *Men of the Global South: A Reader*, London and New York: Zed, 2006.

34 Jorge Larraín, *Identity and Modernity in Latin America*, Cambridge: Polity; and Oxford: Blackwell, 2000, p. 200.

35 Gustavo Gutiérrez, 'Option for the Poor', in Ellacuría and Sobrino (eds), *Mysterium liberationis*, pp. 235–50, at p. 235.

Chapter 1

36 Thomas Cullinan, 'Where the Eucharist Takes Off', in Alistair Kee (ed.), *Seeds of Liberation: Spiritual Dimensions to Political Struggle*, London: SCM Press, 1973, pp. 98–105, at p. 99.

37 Gustavo Gutiérrez, 'Option for the Poor', in Ignacio Ellacuría and Jon Sobrino (eds), *Mysterium liberationis: Fundamental Concepts of Liberation Theology*, Maryknoll, NY: Orbis and Blackburn, Victoria: CollinsDove, 1993, pp. 235–50, at p. 235.

38 Gutiérrez, 'Option for the Poor', p. 235.

39 Juan Luis Segundo SJ, 'Two Theologies of Liberation', Toronto 22 March 1983, in Alfred T. Hennelly (ed.), *Liberation Theology: A Documentary History*, Maryknoll, NY: Orbis, 1990, pp. 353–66.

40 Pablo Richard, 'Theology in the Theology of Liberation', in Ellacuría and Sobrino (eds), *Mysterium liberationis*, pp. 150–68, at p. 152.

41 João B. Libânio, 'Praxis/Orthopraxis', in Virginia Fabella, M. M. Sugirtharajah and R. S. Sugirtharajah (eds), *Dictionary of Third World Theologies*, Maryknoll, NY: Orbis, 2000, pp. 172–3, at p. 172.

42 In the case of the Old Testament this paradigm of preference for the poor by God has been outlined by Juan Alfaro, 'God Protects and Liberates the Poor – O.T.', in Leonardo Boff and Virgil Elizondo (eds), *Option for the Poor: Challenge to the Rich Countries* (*Concilium* 1986/5), Edinburgh: T&T Clark, pp. 27–35.

43 Ronaldo Muñoz, 'God the Father', in Ellacuría and Sobrino (eds), *Mysterium liberationis*, pp. 404–20, at p. 408.

44 Ronaldo Muñoz, *The God of Christians*, Liberation and Theology 11, Tunbridge Wells: Burns & Oates, 1991, p. 88.

45 Pablo Richard et al., *The Idols of Death and the God of Life: A Theology*, Maryknoll, NY: Orbis, 1983.

46 See Maximiliano Salinas Campos, *Don Enrique Alvear: el obispo de los pobres*, Santiago: Ediciones Paulinas, 1991.

47 Elsa Tamez, *The Amnesty of Grace: Justification by Faith from a Latin American Perspective*, Nashville, TN: Abingdon Press, 1993, p. 166.

48 John Petrie (ed.), *The Worker-Priests: A Collective Documentation*, London: Routledge & Kegan Paul, 1956, p. xi.

49 Desmond Doig, *Mother Teresa: Her People and Her Work*, New York: Harper & Row, 1976; and Michael Collopy, *Works of Love Are Works of Peace: Mother Teresa of Calcutta and the Missionaries of Charity*, San Francisco: Ignatius Press, 1996.

50 Leonardo Boff, *When Theology Listens to the Poor*, San Francisco: Harper & Row, 1988, p. 55.

51 I am grateful to Tami Victoria Fernández Cueto, from Oklahoma, currently working in Chile, for pointing out this social reality when I asked her who were the marginalized in Chile today (Tami Fernández to Mario I. Aguilar, 26 April 2007).

52 Aida Edemariam, 'The Undefeated', *Guardian Review* 28 April 2007, p. 11.

53 See Pablo Richard, *Death of Christendoms, Birth of the Church*, Maryknoll, NY: Orbis, 1987.

54 Nelly Richard, 'Cultural Peripheries: Latin America and Post-modernist De-centering', in John Beverley, José Oviedo and Michael Aronna (eds), *The Postmodernist Debate in Latin America*, Durham and London: Duke University Press, 1995, pp. 217–22, at pp. 218–19.

55 Hernán Vidal, 'Postmodernism, Postleftism, and Neo-Avant-Gardism: The Case of Chile's *Revista de Crítica Cultural*', in Beverley, Oviedo and Aronna (eds), *Postmodernist Debate in Latin America*, pp. 282–306, at pp. 282–3; see also Hernán Vidal, *El movimiento contra la tortura Sebastián Acevedo: Derechos humanos y la producción de símbolos nacionales bajo el fascismo chileno*, Santiago: Mosquito Editores, 2002.

56 For a good historical account of Chávez's political career and affiliations with the Cuban leader Fidel Castro, see Richard Gott, *Hugo Chávez and the Bolivarian Revolution*, London and New York: Verso, 2005; for speeches by Chávez, see Hugo Chávez, *Discursos fundamentales: Ideología y acción política, Volume I: 1999*, Caracas: Foro Bolivariano de Nuestra América, 2003, and *The Fascist Coup Against Venezuela: Speeches and Addresses December 2002–January 2003*, La Havana: Ediciones Plaza, 2003.

57 The articles related to indigenous rights within the 1999 Venezuelan Constitution are in Chapter VIII § 119–26.

Chapter 2

58 This was a common challenge for the so-called Third World. African scholars responded systematically within one single volume: see Gerald O. West and Musa W. Dube (eds), *The Bible in Africa: Transactions, Trajectories and Trends*, Leiden, Boston and Cologne: Brill, 2000.

59 Gilberto da Silva Gorgulho, 'Biblical Hermeneutics', in Ignacio Ellacuría and Jon Sobrino (eds), *Mysterium liberationis: Fundamental Concepts of Liberation Theology*, Maryknoll, NY: Orbis; and Blackburn, Victoria: CollinsDove, 1993, pp. 123–50, at p. 124.

60 Silva Gorgulho, 'Biblical Hermeneutics', p. 125; on the general theme of contextual biblical hermeneutics, see J. Severino Croatto, *Biblical Hermeneutics: Towards a Theory of Reading as the Production of Meaning*, Maryknoll, NY: Orbis, 1985.

61 Carlos Mesters, 'The Use of the Bible in Christian Communities of the Common People', in Alfred T. Hennelly (ed.), *Liberation Theology: A Documentary History*, Maryknoll, NY: Orbis, 1990, pp. 14–28, at p. 16.

62 Mesters, 'Use of the Bible in Christian Communities of the Common People' and *Defenseless Flower: A New Reading of the Bible*, Maryknoll, NY: Orbis, 1989.

63 Jung Mo Sung, 'The Human Being as Subject: Defending the Victims', in Iván Petrella (ed.), *Latin American Liberation Theology: The Next Generation*, Maryknoll, NY: Orbis, 2005, pp. 1–19, at pp. 10–11. On the idea of God's love, disorder and life within salvation history, see José Comblin, *Cristãos rumo ao século XXI: Nova caminhada de libertação*, São Paulo: Paulus, 1996.

64 Marcella María Althaus-Reid, 'On Dying Hard: Lessons from Popular Crucifixions and Undisciplined Resurrections in Latin America', in Andrés Torres Queiruga, Luiz Carlos Susin and Jon Sobrino (eds), *The Resurrection of the Dead* (*Concilium* 2006/5), London: SCM Press, pp. 35–43, at p. 39.

65 Marcella María Althaus-Reid, 'From Liberation Theology to Indecent Theology: The Trouble with Normality in Theology', in Petrella (ed.), *Latin American Liberation Theology*, pp. 20–38, at p. 21.

66 Leif E. Vaage, *Subversive Scriptures: Revolutionary Readings of the Christian Bible in Latin America*, Valley Forge, PA: Trinity Press International, 1997.

67 Faustino Teixeira, 'Stories of Faith and Life in the Base Communities', in José Oscar Beozzo and Luiz Carlos Susin (eds), *Brazil: People and Church[es]* (*Concilium* 2002/3), London: SCM Press, pp. 39–46, at p. 42.

68 Sean Freyne, *Galilee, Jesus and the Gospels: Literary Approaches and Historical Investigations*, Philadelphia: Fortress Press, 1988, 'Introduction'.

69 Among the classical works one can mention Martin Hengel, *Judaism and Hellenism*, 2 vols, trans. John Bowden, London: SCM Press, 1974; Hengel, *The Charismatic Leader and His Followers*, Edinburgh: T&T Clark, 1981; and Hengel, *Studies in the Gospel of*

Mark, London: SCM Press, 1985; and the superb survey of Galilee in Richard A. Horsley, *Galilee: History, Politics, People*, Valley Forge, PA: Trinity Press International, 1995.

70 Freyne, *Galilee, Jesus and the Gospels*, p. 269.

71 Michael Holquist (ed.), *The Dialogic Imagination: Four Essays by M. M. Bakhtin*, Austin: University of Texas Press, 1981.

72 Holquist (ed.), *Dialogic Imagination*, p. xix.

73 Gary Saul Morson (ed.), *Bakhtin: Essays and Dialogues on His Work*, Chicago and London: University of Chicago Press, 1986, p. 7.

74 Michael Holquist, *Dialogism: Bakhtin and His World*, London and New York: Routledge, 1990, pp. 20–1.

75 Paul Ricoeur, 'The Model of the Text: Meaningful Action Considered as Text', in Paul Rabinow and William Sullivan (eds), *Interpretive Social Science: A Reader*, Berkeley: University of California Press, 1979, pp. 73–102.

76 R. S. Sugirtharajah, 'Vernacular Resurrections: An Introduction', in R. S. Sugirtharajah (ed.), *Vernacular Hermeneutics*, Sheffield: Sheffield Academic Press, 1999, pp. 11–17, at p. 12.

77 Richard A. Horsley, *Jesus and Empire: The Kingdom of God and the New World Disorder*, Minneapolis, MN: Fortress Press, 2003, p. 72.

78 Fernando Belo, *A Materialistic Reading of the Gospel of Mark*, Maryknoll, NY: Orbis, 1981; and Michel Clevenot, *Materialistic Approaches to the Bible*, Maryknoll, NY: Orbis, 1985; cf. Christopher Rowland, 'The Theology of Liberation and Its Gift to Exegesis', *New Blackfriars* 65, 1984, pp. 157–9.

79 Horsley, *Jesus and Empire*, p. 6.

80 Marcus J. Borg, *Conflict, Holiness & Politics in the Teachings of Jesus*, New York and Toronto: Edwin Mellen Press, 1984, p. 237.

81 For a discussion on the Donatists and the social sciences contra Milbank, see the interpretation of ethnic diversity within liberation theology forwarded by Maldonado-Torres, commenting on the contribution by Gregory Baum: Nelson Maldonado-Torres, 'Liberation Theology and the Search for the Lost Paradigm: From Radical Orthodoxy to Radical Diversality', in Petrella (ed.), *Latin American Liberation Theology*, pp. 39–61, at pp. 48–50.

82 I distinguish here between 'popular religiosity' as a public expression of popular piety within Catholicism and 'popular religion' as an expression of indigenous and popular symbols within a larger system of an inculturated Latin American Christianity as outlined by Diego Irarrázaval, 'Popular Religion', in Virginia Fabella and R. S. Sugirtharajah (eds), *Dictionary of Third World Theologies*, Maryknoll, NY: Orbis, 2000, pp. 167–9.

83 Elsa Támez, *The Amnesty of Grace: Justification by Faith from a*

Notes

Latin American Perspective, Nashville, TN: Abingdon Press, 1993, p. 163.

84 Althaus-Reid, 'From Liberation Theology to Indecent Theology', p. 21.

85 Christopher Rowland and Mark Corner, *Liberating Exegesis: The Challenge of Liberation Theology to Biblical Studies*, Louisville, KY: Westminster/John Knox Press, 1989, pp. 7–17; for a critique of Rowland and Corner, see Marcella Althaus-Reid, *From Feminist Theology to Indecent Theology: Readings on Poverty, Sexual Identity and God*, London: SCM Press, 2004, pp. 137–8.

86 Jon Sobrino sj, *Christology at the Crossroads: A Latin American Approach*, London: SCM Press, 1978, pp. 179–272, and *Jesus the Liberator: A Historical-Theological Reading of Jesus of Nazareth*, Tunbridge Wells: Burns & Oates, 1994, pp. 233–71; and Althaus-Reid, *From Feminist Theology to Indecent Theology*, pp. 172–6.

87 The Roman coin, the silver denarius – worth a daily wage (Mt. 20.2) – had the image of the emperor on it, following a Roman practice of engraving human likeness, a practice that was rejected by the Jews (Exodus 20.3), who used small copper coins. If commentators are correct, and the coin was minted by Tiberius in the 20s CE, its legend read TI CAESAR DIVI AVG F AVGVSTVS – Tiberius Caesar Augustus, Son of Divine Augustus, thus proclaiming the divinity of the Roman emperor: see Craig A. Evans, *Mark 8:27–16:20*, World Biblical Commentary, Vol. 34 B, Nashville, TN: Thomas Nelson, 2001, p. 247.

88 The Romans had imposed forced taxation (χήνσος) in 6 CE when Judea, Samaria and Idumea were placed under Roman occupation. Judas and others revolted against such taxation (Acts 5.37) that implied the partition of Jewish land, a policy that led to the creation of the Zealot movement and the rising of 70 CE (Josephus, *Antiquities* XVIII:1.1,6). It was therefore unlawful to suggest that taxes to Rome were not to be paid and it was contentious within a Jewish milieu to suggest that taxes to the oppressors should be paid.

89 Carlos Bravo, 'Jesus of Nazareth, Christ the Liberator', in Ellacuría and Sobrino (eds), *Mysterium liberationis*, pp. 420–39, at p. 433.

90 Mario I. Aguilar, 'Rethinking the Judean Past: Questions of History and a Social Archaeology of Memory in the First Book of the Maccabees', *Biblical Theology Bulletin* 30, 2000, pp. 58–67.

91 Michel Foucault, *The Archaeology of Knowledge*, London and New York: Routledge, [1970] 1980, p. 11.

92 Michael Taussig, *Mimesis and Alterity: A Particular History of the Senses*, New York and London: Routledge, 1993, p. xiii.

93 Borg refers to the 'framework' as 'an eschatological mysticism': see Borg, *Conflict, Holiness & Politics in the Teachings of Jesus*, p. 261.

Chapter 3

94 Ernesto Cardenal, *El Evangelio en Solentiname*, Salamanca: Ediciones Sígueme, 1976, and *El Evangelio en Solentiname: Volumen Segundo*, Salamanca: Ediciones Sígueme, 1978.

95 Néstor Oscar Míguez, 'Hermeneutical Circle', in Virginia Fabella and R. S. Sugirtharajah (eds), *Dictionary of Third World Theologies*, Maryknoll, NY: Orbis, 2000, p. 97.

96 The Spanish word is *caminata*, used within Latin American theology to indicate the process of doing theology within a community and an ongoing walk as a member of a particular community: see Marcella Althaus-Reid, *From Feminist Theology To Indecent Theology*, London: SCM Press, 2004, p. 12 note 1.

97 If the use of Marxism in order to read reality and the biblical text dominated the foundations and early start of liberation theologies, other social sciences, cultural theory and even psychoanalysis have been areas to explore the possibility of doing theology from the standpoint of the victims without allowing such theologies to become European in method and epistemology: see an interesting critique of the early theology of liberation regarding the use of the social sciences in Manuel J. Mejido, 'Beyond the Postmodern Condition, or the Turn towards Psychoanalysis', in Iván Petrella (ed.), *Latin American Liberation Theology: The Next Generation*, Maryknoll, NY: Orbis, 2005, pp. 119–46. For some important ideas that have contributed to the use of the social sciences in the study of religion and the development of theology, see Richard H. Roberts, 'Theology and the Social Sciences', in Erik Borgman and Felix Wilfred (eds), *Theology in a World of Specialization* (*Concilium* 2006/2), London: SCM Press, pp. 122–30.

98 For a more contemporary assessment of the margins and the marginal, see Joerg Rieger (ed.), *Opting for the Margins: Postmodernity and Liberation in Christian Theology*, Oxford: Oxford University Press, 2003.

99 Jung Mo Sung, 'The Human Being as Subject: Defending the Victims', in Petrella (ed.), *Latin American Liberation Theology*, pp. 1–19, at pp. 4–5.

100 I am conscious here that personally I have had experiences of particular peripheries throughout my life and I take on board the moving peripheries of migrants as subjects, 'because migrants are both economic actors and agents in the production of culture': see Nancy E. Bedford, 'To Speak of God from More Than One Place: Theological Reflections from the Experience of Migration', in Petrella (ed.), *Latin American Liberation Theology*, pp. 95–118, at p. 96.

101 Daniel M. Bell Jr, *Liberation Theology after the End of History:*

Notes

The Refusal to Cease Suffering, London: Routledge, 2001.

102 Timothy C. Champion, 'Introduction', in T. C. Champion (ed.), *Centre and Periphery: Comparative Studies in Archaeology*, London and New York: Routledge, 1995, pp. 1–21; J. Gottmann, *Centre and Periphery: Spatial Variations in Politics*, Beverly Hills and London: Sage, 1980; Enrique Dussel, 'Theologies of the "Periphery" and the "Centre": Encounter or Confrontation?', in Claude Geffré, Gustavo Gutiérrez and Virgil Elizondo (eds), *Different Theologies, Common Responsibility, Babel or Pentecost?* (*Concilium* 1984/1), Edinburgh: T&T Clark, pp. 87–97.

103 Dussel, 'Theologies of the "Periphery" and the "Centre"', p. 94.

104 Ignacio Ellacuría and Jon Sobrino (eds), *Mysterium liberationis: Fundamental Concepts of Liberation Theology*, Maryknoll, NY: Orbis; and Blackburn, Victoria: CollinsDove, 1993.

105 Clodovis Boff, *Teología de lo politico: Sus mediaciones*, Salamanca: Sígueme, 1980.

106 Marcella María Althaus-Reid, 'Who Framed Clodovis Boff? Revisiting the Controversy of "Theologies of the Genitive" in the Twenty-First Century', in Borgman and Wilfred (eds), *Theology in a World of Specialization*, pp. 99–107, at pp. 99–100.

107 Althaus-Reid, 'Who Framed Clodovis Boff?', p. 103.

108 Uriel Molina Oliú, 'How a People's Christian Community (Comunidad Cristiana Popular) is Structured and How It Functions', in Leonardo Boff and Virgil Elizondo (eds), *La Iglesia Popular: Between Fear and Hope* (*Concilium* 1984/6), Edinburgh: T&T Clark, pp. 3–9, at p. 5.

109 Vered Amit, 'Reconceptualizing Community', in Vered Amit (ed.), *Realizing Community: Concepts, Social Relationships and Sentiments*, London and New York: Routledge, 2002, pp. 1–20, at p. 18.

110 In the case of Brazil, the country not only has the largest number of Roman Catholics but also the largest number of Pentecostals in the world: see 'The Tablet Interview: Unlikely Bureaucrat', an interview with Cardinal Cláudio Hummes, head of the Vatican Congregation for the Clergy, *The Tablet* 12 May 2007, pp. 12–13.

111 Benedict XVI on his arrival in Brazil said: 'I am happy to be able to spend some days among the Brazilian people. I am well aware that the soul of this people, as of all Latin America, safeguards values that are radically Christian, which will never be eradicated. I am certain that at Aparecida, during the Bishops' General Conference, this identity will be reinforced through the promotion of respect for life from the moment of conception until natural death as an integral requirement of human nature. It will also make the promotion of the human person the axis of solidarity, especially towards the poor and abandoned' (Speech of

197

Benedict XVI on his arrival at Guarulhos Airport, São Paulo, 9 May 2007).

112 A good example of that inscription of individual voices can be found in Eva Montes de Oca, *Guía negra de Buenos Aires: Marginación en la gran ciudad*, Buenos Aires: Planeta, 1995.

113 José Comblin, *Called for Freedom: The Changing Context of Liberation Theology*, Maryknoll, NY: Orbis, 1998, p. 211.

114 For an excellent overview of a Latin American theological anthropology, see José Ignacio González Faus, 'Anthropology: The Person and the Community', in Ellacuría and Sobrino (eds), *Mysterium liberationis*, pp. 497–521.

115 Faus, 'Anthropology', p. 497.

116 Benedict XVI, Address to the Brazilian Bishops, Catedral da Sé, São Paulo, 11 May 2007.

117 That role had not previously changed but the Brazilian bishops particularly had changed the centre–periphery structures of the Catholic Church in Brazil by allowing the Basic Christian Communities through their leaders and catechists to explore issues of faith and doctrine in their local contexts. The diocesan structures implemented by the Brazilian bishops gave less importance to the bureaucratic centres at bishops' offices and stressed the location of the centres of catechesis within the periphery, thus within the daily life of communities and of the Brazilian Basic Christian Communities. See, for example, Alois Lorscheider, 'The Re-Defined Role of the Bishop in a Poor, Religious People (*Meio Popular Pobre e Religioso*)', in Boff and Elizondo (eds), *La Iglesia Popular*, pp. 47–9.

118 'Editorial: Brazil's Challenge to Benedict', *The Tablet* 12 May 2007, p. 2.

119 Robert Mickens, 'Letter from São Paulo', *The Tablet* 12 May 2007, p. 34.

Chapter 4

120 Avery Dulles SJ, *Models of the Church: A Critical Assessment of the Church in All Its Aspects*, Dublin: Gill & Macmillan, 1976, p. 8.

121 Dulles SJ, *Models of the Church*, p. 9.

122 *Ad Gentes Divinitus* § 5.

123 On the basis of this theological pluralism and the role of the Christian community, see Jean-Marie Tillard OP, 'Theological Pluralism and the Mystery of the Church', in Claude Geffré, Gustavo Gutiérrez and Virgil Elizondo (eds), *Different Theologies, Common Responsibility, Babel or Pentecost?* (*Concilium* 1984/1), Edinburgh: T&T Clark, pp. 62–73.

124 Sallie McFague, *Models of God: Theology for an Ecological Nuclear Age*, London: SCM Press, 1987, p. 139.

125 *Gaudium et Spes* § 1.

126 *Lumen Gentium* § 12.

127 *Lumen Gentium* § 12–13.

128 *Lumen Gentium* §16.

129 *Lumen Gentium* §16.

130 This was an important factor in the influence of the Christian communities on the bishops' deliberations at Medellín: see, for example, Luiz Alberto Gómez de Souza, 'The Origins of Medellín: From Catholic Action to the Base Church Communities and Social Pastoral Strategy (1950–68)', in José Oscar Beozzo and Luiz Carlos Susin (eds), *Brazil: People and Church[es]* (*Concilium* 2002/3), London: SCM Press, pp. 31–7.

131 Sunday, 13 May 2007.

132 The Latin American bishops use the word 'sect' in order to describe those groups who have not a central doctrinal body of authority, thus it is difficult to know what they actually believe; mention of them is made in the documents of Puebla § 628 and Santo Domingo § 12. See John Eagleson and Philip Scharper (eds), *Puebla and Beyond: Documentation and Commentary*, Maryknoll, NY: Orbis, 1979; and Alfred Hennelly (ed.), *Santo Domingo and Beyond: Documents and Commentaries from the Historic Meeting of the Latin American Bishops' Conference*, Maryknoll, NY: Orbis, 1993. For further analysis of those groups, see: Brenda Maribel Carranza Dávila, 'Pentecostal Flames in Contemporary Brazil', in Beozzo and Susin (eds), *Brazil*, pp. 93–101; R. Andrew Chesnut, *Born again in Brazil: The Pentecostal Boom and the Pathogens of Poverty*, New Brunswick, NJ: Rutgers University Press, 1997; Ricardo Mariano, *Neopentecostais, sociologia do novo pentecostalismo no Brasil*, São Paulo: Loyola, 1999; and Reginaldo Prandi, *Un sopro do espíritu*, São Paulo: EDUSP-FABESP.

133 In these discussions, I appreciate that the initial efforts by Gustavo Gutiérrez to ground a theology of liberation and issues related to the Kingdom of God on the developments of a council, Vatican II, were sound. Jon Sobrino remarked that Gutiérrez had not dealt with the biblical foundation of the Kingdom of God, a task that Sobrino undertook later: see Jon Sobrino sj, *Jesus the Liberator: A Historical-Theological Reading of Jesus of Nazareth*, Tunbridge Wells: Burns & Oates, 1994, pp. 122–34. Regarding the interpretation of the biblical text, there could be many ways of hermeneutical aggiornamento but in times of theological disagreement theologians, and Benedict XVI as one of them, return within the Catholic tradition to the councils, the encyclicals and the Fathers of the Church.

134 Sobrino SJ, *Jesus the Liberator*, p. 122.

135 Gustavo Gutiérrez, 'Speaking About God', in Geffré, Gutiérrez and Elizondo (eds), *Different Theologies*, pp. 27–31, at p. 31.

136 *Dignitatis Humanae* § 3.

137 Dulles SJ, *Models of the Church*, pp. 83, 86.

138 *Gaudium et Spes* § 93.

139 See Santo Domingo § 62–3; note that the Brazilian Cardinal Cláudio Hummes, Head of the Vatican Congregation for the Clergy and previously Archbishop of São Paulo, expressed such reality by stating that 'History moves forward and we must move with history, otherwise we will keep sliding into the past . . . The Church's presence among the poor continues today and very strongly, albeit a bit less ideological and less political' ('The Tablet Interview: Unlikely Bureaucrat', *The Tablet* 12 May 2007, pp. 12–13 at p. 13).

140 Daniel M. Bell Jr, *Liberation Theology after the End of History: The Refusal to Cease Suffering*, London: Routledge, 2001.

141 Iván Petrella, *The Future of Liberation Theology: An Argument and Manifesto*, Aldershot and Burlington, VT: Ashgate, 2004, pp. 128–32.

142 See: John Milbank, *Theology and Social Theory: Beyond Secular Reason*, Oxford: Blackwell, 1990; Stanley Hauerwas and William Willimon, *Resident Aliens: Life in the Christian Colony*, Nashville, TN: Abingdon Press, 1989; Stanley Hauerwas, *A Better Hope: Resources for a Church Confronting Capitalism, Democracy and Postmodernity*, Michigan: Brazos Press, 2000; and 'Some Theological Reflections on Gutiérrez's Use of "Liberation" as a Theological Concept', *Modern Theology* 3, 1, 1986, pp. 67–76.

143 Dulles SJ, *Models of the Church*, p. 95.

144 Libânio mentions the 'Cry of the Excluded' movement within civil society on the Brazilian National Day, the 'National Plebiscite on External Debt' that took place in Brazil from 2 to 7 September 2000, and the 'Brotherhood Campaign', all initiatives of the Catholic Church working closely together with other civil organizations: see Joâo Batista Libânio, 'Pastoral Strategy in the Brazilian Mega-Cities', in Beozzo and Susin (eds), *Brazil*, pp. 61–70, at p. 68.

145 Ignacio Ellacuría, 'The Political Nature of Jesus' Mission', in José Miguez Bonino (ed.), *Faces of Jesus: Latin American Christologies*, Eugene, OR: Wipf & Stock, 1998, pp. 79–92, at p. 91.

146 Gustavo Gutiérrez, *The God of Life*, London: SCM Press, 1991, p. 2.

147 Norman Kember, *Hostage in Iraq*, London: Darton, Longman & Todd, 2007, p. 192.

148 Jon Sobrino SJ, *Jesus the Liberator*, pp. 254–71, and 'Redeeming

Notes

Globalization through Its Victims', in Jon Sobrino and Felix Wilfred (eds), *Globalization and Its Victims* (*Concilium* 2001/5), London: SCM Press, pp. 105–14.

149 Marcella Althaus-Reid, *Indecent Theology: Theological Perversions in Sex, Gender and Politics*, London: Routledge, 2000.

Chapter 5

150 Benedict XVI, 'Address to the Bishops of Brazil in the Catedral da Sé', 11 May 2007, § 6.

151 I have explored the sociology of Pentecostalism in the Introduction to *The History and Politics of Latin American Theology*, Volume I, London: SCM Press, 2007. See also: David Martin, *Tongues of Fire: The Explosion of Protestantism in Latin America*, Oxford: Basil Blackwell, 1990; and David Stoll, *Is Latin America Turning Protestant? The Politics of Evangelical Growth*, Berkeley: University of California Press, 1990.

152 Margaret Hebblethwaite, 'Continent of Hope', *The Tablet* 19 May 2007, p. 14.

153 Felix Wilfred argues that three important theological readings are necessary to understand the efforts by Western theologians to save a depleting Christianity in the North, namely, neo-orthodoxy, neoliberal theology and a postmodernist reading. None of them works because their paradigm pro-capitalism has not managed to save Christianity from secularism in the North while Christianity continues growing in the South: see Felix Wilfred, 'Christianity between Decline and Resurgence', in Jon Sobrino and Felix Wilfred (eds), *Christianity in Crisis?* (*Concilium* 2005/3), London: SCM Press, pp. 27–37, at pp. 29–32; compare those arguments with the Latin American analysis in Leonardo Boff, *Global Civilization: Challenges to Society and Christianity*, London: Equinox, 2005, and José Comblin, *Called for Freedom: The Changing Context of Liberation Theology*, Maryknoll, NY: Orbis, 1998.

154 Adolfo Nicolás, 'Christianity in Crisis: Asia. Which Asia? Which Christianity? Which Crisis?', in Sobrino and Wilfred (eds), *Christianity in Crisis?*, pp. 64–70, at p. 65.

155 Eduardo de la Serna, 'The Crisis of Christianity in Latin America', in Sobrino and Wilfred (eds), *Christianity in Crisis?*, pp. 84–8, at p. 87.

156 In the case of Africa, Ludovic Lado sj has argued that 'Catholicism and Pentecostalism are going to have to engage in dialogue in Africa because many African families are *de facto* ecumenical': see Ludovic Lado sj, 'African Catholicism in the Face of Pentecostalism', in

Éloi Messi Metogo (ed.), *African Christianities* (*Concilium* 2006/4), London: SCM Press, pp. 22–9, at p. 29.

157 *Unitatis Redintegratio* § 1.

158 *Unitatis Redintegratio* § 21.

159 José Comblin, 'Experiences of Crisis in the History of Christianity', in Sobrino and Wilfred (eds), *Christianity in Crisis?*, pp. 97–107, at p. 107.

160 Margaret Hebblethwaite, 'Continent of Hope', *The Tablet* 19 May 2007, p. 14.

161 Jürgen Manemann, 'The Permanence of the Theological-Political Opportunities and Threats for Christianity in the Current Crisis of Democracy', in Sobrino and Wilfred (eds), *Christianity in Crisis?*, pp. 48–58, at p. 49.

162 Leonardo Boff speaks of 'Roman Catholic fundamentalism', in *Fundamentalism, Terrorism and the Future of Humanity*, London: SPCK, 2006, p. 9.

163 Santo Domingo §§ 26, 38, 133, 139, 140, 141, 146, 147, 148, 280.

164 See, for example, Rebecca Pierce Bomann, *Faith in the Barrios: The Pentecostal Poor in Bogotá*, Boulder and London: Lynne Rienner Publishers, 1999.

165 Jon Sobrino, 'Crisis and God', in Sobrino and Wilfred (eds), *Christianity in Crisis?*, pp. 115–24, at p. 123.

166 *Lumen Gentium* § 9.

167 Comblin, *Called for Freedom*, p. 114.

168 Walter J. Hollenweger, *Pentecostalism: Origins and Developments Worldwide*, Peabody, MA: Hendrickson, 1997, p. 19.

169 Hollenweger, *Pentecostalism*, p. 20.

170 Jorge Larraín, *Identity and Modernity in Latin America*, Cambridge: Polity, 2000.

171 For an interesting reflection on Pentecostalism and identity, see Guillermo Cook, 'Interchurch Relations: Exclusion, Ecumenism, and the Poor', in Edward L. Cleary and Hannah W. Stewart-Gambino (eds), *Power, Politics, and Pentecostals in Latin America*, Boulder, CO: Westview, 1998, pp. 77–96, and Cook's edited collection, *New Face of the Church in Latin America: Between Tradition and Change*, Maryknoll, NY: Orbis, 1994.

172 André Corten and Ruth Marshall-Fratani (eds), *Between Babel and Pentecost: Transnational Pentecostalism in Africa and Latin America*, Bloomington and Indianapolis: Indiana University Press, 2001.

173 Hollenweger, *Pentecostalism*, p. 167.

174 Simon Chan, *Pentecostal Theology and the Christian Spiritual Tradition*, Journal of Pentecostal Theology Supplement Series 21,

Sheffield: Sheffield Academic Press, 2000, p. 98.

175 Chan, *Pentecostal Theology*, p. 99.

176 *Pastoralia* 7/15 December 1985, special issue on 'Pentecostalismo y teología de la liberación', cited in Hollenweger, *Pentecostalism*, p. 209.

177 Hollenweger, *Pentecostalism*, p. 370.

178 Hollenweger, *Pentecostalism*, p. 400.

179 Boff, *Fundamentalism*, p. 70.

180 José María Vigil, 'The Pluralist Paradigm: Tasks for Theology toward a Pluralist Re-reading of Christianity', in Andrés Torres Queirug, Luiz Carlos Susin and José María Vigil (eds), *Pluralist Theology: The Emerging Paradigm* (*Concilium* 2007/1), London: SCM Press, pp. 31–9, at p. 36.

181 Marcelo Barros, 'Dwellings of the Wind on Human Paths: Toward a Theology of Hiero-diversity', in Queirug, Susin and Vigil (eds), *Pluralist Theology*, pp. 49–56, at p. 53.

Chapter 6

182 Leonardo Boff, *Francisco de Assis: Ternura e vigor – Uma leitura a partir dos pobres*, Petrópolis: Editora Vozes, 1981, and *Francisco de Assis: Homem do paraíso*, Petrópolis: Editora Vozes, 1985.

183 See Mario I. Aguilar, *The History and Politics of Latin American Theology*, Volume I, London: SCM Press, 2007, chapter 5. Ernesto Cardenal, *El Evangelio en Solentiname*, Salamanca: Ediciones Sígueme, 1976, and *El Evangelio en Solentiname: Volumen Segundo*, Salamanca: Ediciones Sígueme, 1978.

184 See, for example, Elsa Tamez, 'I Timothy and James on the Rich, Women, and Theological Disputes', in Sean Freyne and Ellen van Wolde (eds), *The Many Voices of the Bible* (*Concilium* 2002/1), London: SCM Press, pp. 49–58.

185 The 14th Dalai Lama, 'The Nobel Peace Prize Lecture, Oslo, Norway', in Sidney Piburn (ed.), *The Dalai Lama: A Policy of Kindness – An Anthology of Writings by and about the Dalai Lama*, Ithaca, NY: Snow Lion Publications, 1990, pp. 15–25, at p. 15. The connections between Thomas Merton and the Dalai Lama are important because Ernesto Cardenal and the new foundation of the Trappist monastery in Santiago were all connected through discourses that arose out of the influence of Merton on the American interfaith dialogue and later on the Latin American challenges to violence, particularly at the time of the military regimes; see, for example, Joseph Quinn Raab, 'Comrades for Peace: Thomas Merton, the Dalai Lama and the Preferential Option for Nonviolence', in Victor A. Kramer and David Belcastro (eds), *The*

Merton Annual: Studies in Culture, Spirituality and Social Concerns 19, Louisville, KY: Fons Vitae, 2006, pp. 255–66.

186 Ignacio Ellacuría, *Freedom Made Flesh: The Mission of Christ and His Church*, Maryknoll, NY: Orbis, 1976, pp. 1–19.

187 Jon Sobrino, 'Spirituality and the Following of Jesus', in Ignacio Ellacuría and Jon Sobrino (eds), *Mysterium liberationis: Fundamental Concepts of Liberation Theology*, Maryknoll, NY; and Blackburn, Victoria: Orbis and Collins Dove, 1993, pp. 677–701, at p. 677.

188 See, for example, the insightful analysis of the Gospels vis-à-vis Latin American society by J. Severino Croatto, 'The Political Dimension of Christ the Liberator', in José Miguez Bonino (ed.), *Faces of Jesus: Latin American Christologies*, Eugene, OR: Wipf & Stock, 1998, pp. 102–22.

189 Jon Sobrino, 'Central Position of the Reign of God in Liberation Theology', in Ellacuría and Sobrino (eds), *Mysterium liberationis*, pp. 350–88, at pp. 378–9.

190 For the development of a global ethics within centre-theologies, see Hans Küng, 'Global Business and the Global Ethic', in Karl-Josef Kuschel and Dietmar Mieth (eds), *In Search of Universal Values* (*Concilium* 2001/4), London: SCM Press, pp. 87–105.

191 Ola Sigurdson, 'Songs of Desire: On Pop-Music and the Question of God', in Werner Jeanrond and Christoph Theobald (eds), *God: Experience and Mystery* (*Concilium* 2001/1), London: SCM Press, pp. 34–42, at p. 41.

192 William T. Cavanaugh, 'Consumption, the Market, and the Eucharist', in Christophe Boureux, Janet Martin Soskice and Luiz Carlos Susin (eds), *Hunger, Bread and Eucharist* (*Concilium* 2005/2), London: SCM Press, pp. 88–95, at p. 94.

193 For a contemporary globalized view of global inequality, see Iván Petrella, 'Liberation Theology: A Programmatic Statement', in Iván Petrella (ed.), *Latin American Liberation Theology: The Next Generation*, Maryknoll, NY: Orbis, 2005, pp. 147–72.

194 Santo Domingo § 37.

195 *Perfectae Caritatis* § 15.

196 Santo Domingo § 86.

197 See, for example, Dorothee Soelle, *The Silent Cry: Mysticism and Resistance*, Minneapolis, MN: Fortress Press, 2001.

198 Thomas Merton wanted to relocate to Latin America, either to the Chilean foundation or to Nicaragua to be in Solentiname with Ernesto Cardenal. On 3 July 1966, Merton wrote to Cardenal: 'You will be interested in the important news that Gethsemani is taking over the Spencer foundation in Chile. This is important because it now means that Gethsemani is engaged in work in Latin America. Some monks are

going down in August and others in October. I do not think I am likely to be sent there but anything may happen' (in Christine M. Bochen (ed.), *Thomas Merton: The Courage for Truth – Letters to Writers*, New York: Farrar, Straus & Giroux, 1993, p. 156).

199 A few years ago the Trappists moved to Rancagua, a city south of Santiago, searching for a quieter place, as the expansion of urban Santiago had reached the vicinity of the their monastery.

200 For theological reflections on the active apostolate of the religious congregations in Latin America, see Jon Sobrino, 'Religious Life in the Third World', *The True Church of the Poor*, London: SCM Press, 1985, pp. 302–37.

201 Pedro Casaldáliga and José María Vigil, *The Spirituality of Liberation*, Liberation and Theology 12, Tunbridge Wells: Burns & Oates, 1994, p. 103.

202 Marcella Althaus-Reid, *From Feminist Theology to Indecent Theology: Readings on Poverty, Sexual Identity and God*, London: SCM Press, 2004, p. 161.

203 Cavanaugh, 'Consumption, the Market, and the Eucharist', p. 91.

204 Hadwig Ana Maria Müller, 'Hunger for Bread – the Desire of the Other', in Boureux, Soskice and Susin (eds), *Hunger, Bread and Eucharist*, pp. 73–9, at p. 76.

205 'Commonalities, Divergences, and Cross-fertilization among Third World Theologies: A Document based on the Seventh International Conference of the Ecumenical Association of Third World Theologians, Oaxtepec, Mexico, December 7–14, 1986', § 65, in K. C. Abraham (ed.), *Third World Theologies: Commonalities and Differences*, Maryknoll, NY: Orbis, 1990, pp. 207–8.

206 Gustavo Gutiérrez, *The God of Life*, London: SCM Press, 1991, p. 189.

Chapter 7

207 Argument developed in Leonardo Boff, *Global Civilization: Challenges to Society and Christianity*, London: Equinox, p. 6, English translation of *Nova era: A civilização Planetária*, São Paulo: Animus/Anima Producoes, 2003; cf. Darcy Ribeiro, *The Civilizational Process*, Washington, DC: Smithsonian Institution Press, 1968.

208 Patrick Claffey, 'Hope or Dope: Christian Churches and Socio-Political Development in Africa', The Africa Lecture delivered at the Centre for the Study of Religion and Politics (CSRP) of the University of St Andrews, 26 April 2007, text available at <http://www.st-andrews.ac.uk/divinity/CSRP%20Hope%20or%20Dope.pdf>.

209 Boff, *Global Civilization*, p. 21.

210 Leonardo Boff, *Fundamentalism, Terrorism and the Future of Humanity*, London: SPCK, 2006, p. 61.

211 *Pacem in Terris*, Encyclical of Pope John XXIII on establishing universal peace in truth, justice, charity and liberty, 11 April 1963.

212 *Pacem in Terris* § 112.

213 Between 1980 and 1984 the US administration gave $400 million in aid, 'still at levels one-fifth lower than in the late 1970s'; see Hugh Byrne, *El Salvador's Civil War: A Study of Revolution*, Boulder and London: Lynne Rienner, 1996, p. 122.

214 Michael Hirsch, John Barry and Mark Hosenball, 'Opción El Salvador para Irak: El Pentágono estudia enviar fuerzas especiales para la creación de Escuadrones de la muerte Iraquíes', *Newsweek/IrakSolidaridad* 14 January 2005.

215 'Soldado caído se perpetúa en Nayaf', *Diario Co Latino* 19 April 2004.

216 'Prevé El Salvador permanencia de tropas en Irak en 2007', *Diario de Chiapas* 28 December 2006.

217 'El Salvador podría enviar más tropas a Irak', *La Prensa Gráfica/Prensa Latina* 1 December 2006.

218 'Luteranos piden que tropas salvadoreñas regresen de Iraq', *Diario Co Latino* 20 April 2004.

219 Mirna Jiménez, 'Sería mejor que El Salvador empezara a desmantelar su contingente: PDDH', *Diario Co Latino* 21 April 2004.

220 'Oposición cuestiona indiferencia de Flores por futuro de tropas', *Diario Co Latino* 20 April 2004.

221 Elson Concepción Pérez, 'El Salvador, Irak . . . y las remesas de la guerra', *Las Dos Habanas/Cuba* 20 July 2004.

222 José Comblin, *Called for Freedom: The Changing Context of Liberation Theology*, Maryknoll, NY: Orbis, 1998, p. 194.

223 *Redemptoris Missio*, Encyclical Letter of John Paul II on the permanent validity of the Church's missionary mandate, 1991, § 82.

224 Santo Domingo §§ 9, 107, 110.

225 See Mario Aguilar, *The History and Politics of Latin American Theology*, Volume I, London: SCM Press, 2007; Volume II, London: SCM Press, 2008.

226 Ginger Thompson, 'The Migrant', from Ginger Thompson, 'The Desperate Risk Death in a Desert', *New York Times* 31 October 2000, in Adam Jones (ed.), *Men of the Global South: A Reader*, London and New York: Zed, 2006, pp. 322–4, at p. 323.

227 Alejandro Torres, 'Ningún muro dividirá a mexicanos, asevera Fox', *El Universal* 6 October 2006; and José Luis Ruiz, 'Fox: le faltó "visión" a EU al avalar el muro', *El Universal* 7 October 2006.

Notes

228 Juan Balboa, 'Condena la EU que Estados Unidos busque edificar muro', *La Jornada* 18 January 2006.

229 Conferencia del Episcopado Mexicano (CEM), 'Entrevista a Monseñor Renato Ascencio León Obispo de Ciudad Juárez, Presidente de la Comisión Episcopal para Pastoral de la Movilidad Humana', 11 May 2005.

230 Cámara de Diputados de México, Primer Receso del Tercer Año de Ejercicio, Sesión No. 3, 11 January 2006.

231 Ivone Gebara, 'Can the Merchants Be Driven out of the Temple of Life? An Ecological Feminist Reflection from Latin America', in Marie-Theres Wacker and Elaine M. Wainwright (eds), *Land Conflicts, Land Utopias* (*Concilium* 2007/2), London: SCM Press, pp. 97–100, at p. 97.

232 James A. Nash, *Loving Nature: Ecological Integrity and Christian Responsibility*, Nasville, TN and Washington, DC: Abingdon Press and The Churches' Center for Theology and Public Policy, 1991, p. 33.

233 Santo Domingo § 9.

234 Boff, *Global Civilization*, p. 75.

235 Leonardo Boff, *Ecology & Liberation: A New Paradigm*, Maryknoll, NY: Orbis, 1995, pp. 43–5; see also John Austin Baker, 'Biblical Views of Nature', in Charles Birch, William Eakin and Jay B. McDaniel (eds), *Liberating Life: Contemporary Approaches to Ecological Theology*, Maryknoll, NY: Orbis, 1990, pp. 9–26, at pp. 10–11.

236 Leonardo Boff, *Cry of the Earth: Cry of the Poor*, Maryknoll, NY: Orbis, 1997, p. 113.

237 Ingemar Hedström, 'Latin America and the Need for a Life-Liberating Theology', in Birch, Eakin and McDaniel (eds), *Liberating Life*, pp. 111–24, at p. 120.

238 Sallie McFague, 'Imaging a Theology of Nature: The World as God's Body', in Birch, Eakin and McDaniel (eds), *Liberating Life*, pp. 201–27, at p. 213. For a full development of this theological argument, see Sallie McFague, *The Body of God: An Ecological Theology*, London: SCM Press, 1993, and for further reflections her paper 'The World as God's Body', in Regina Ammicht-Quinn and Elsa Tamez (eds), *The Body and Religion* (*Concilium* 2002/2), London: SCM Press, pp. 50–6.

239 Seán McDonagh, *Greening the Christian Millennium*, Dublin: Dominican Publications, 1999, p. 72.

Chapter 8

240 María Arcelia Gonzáles Butron, 'The Effects of Free-Market Globalization on Women's Lives', in Jon Sobrino and Felix Wilfred (eds), *Globalization and Its Victims* (*Concilium* 2001/5), London: SCM Press, pp. 43–50.

241 Puebla § 833, cf. §§ 804–5, 811–17; Santo Domingo §§ 96, 99, 101, 179.

242 *Christifideles Laici* § 21–3.

243 Simon Chan, *Pentecostal Theology and the Christian Spiritual Tradition*, Journal of Pentecostal Theology Supplement 21, Sheffield: Sheffield Academic Press, 2000, p. 100.

244 Miroslav Volf, *After Our Likeness: The Church as the Image of the Trinity*, Grand Rapids, MI: Eerdmans, 1998.

245 José Comblin, *Called for Freedom: The Changing Context of Liberation Theology*, Maryknoll, NY: Orbis, 1998, p. 120.

246 See Marcella Althaus-Reid, 'Gustavo Gutiérrez Goes to Disneyland: Theme Park Theologies and the Diaspora of the Discourse of the Popular Theologian in Liberation Theology', *From Feminist Theology to Indecent Theology*, London: SCM Press, 2004, pp. 124–42, at p. 129.

247 Jung Mo Sung, 'The Human Being as Subject: Defending the Victims', in Iván Petrella (ed.), *Latin American Liberation Theology: The Next Generation*, Maryknoll, N.Y. Orbis, 2005, pp. 1–19, at p. 5.

248 Althaus-Reid, *From Feminist Theology to Indecent Theology*, p. 140.

249 See, for example, the anthropological study by Hernán Vidal, *El Movimiento Contra la Tortura Sebastián Acevedo: Derechos humanos y la producción de símbolos nacionales bajo el fascismo chileno*, Santiago, Chile: Mosquito Editores, 2002.

250 The definition of torture followed for this period of Chilean history was that provided by the Chilean National Commission on Truth and Reconciliation, a commission that chose to follow Article 1 of the 'Convention against Torture, and Cruel, Inhuman or Degrading Treatment or Punishment' that reads as follows: 'For the purposes of this Convention, torture means any act by which severe pain or suffering, whether physical or mental, is intentionally inflicted on a person for such purposes as obtaining from him or a third person information or a confession, punishing him for an act he or a third person has committed or is suspected of having committed, or intimidating or coercing him or a third person, or for any reason based on discrimination of any kind, when such pain or suffering is inflicted by or at the instigation of, or with the consent or acquiescence of a public official or other person acting in an official capacity. It does not include pain or suffering arising only

Notes

from, inherent in or incidental to, lawful sanctions' (in *Report of the Chilean National Commission on Truth and Reconciliation* I, Notre Dame: Center for Civil and Human Rights, Notre Dame Law School and University of Notre Dame Press, 1993, pp. 38–9).

251 José Aldunate, 'Prólogo: El Movimiento Contra la Tortura Sebastián Acevedo – Una relación complementaria', in Vidal, *El Movimiento Contra la Tortura Sebastián Acevedo*, pp. 9–27.

252 Ivone Gebara, 'Can the Merchants Be Driven Out of the Temple of Life? An Ecological Feminist Reflection from Latin America', in Marie-Theres Wacker and Elaine M. Wainwright (eds), *Land Conflicts, Land Utopias* (*Concilium* 2007/2), London: SCM Press, pp. 97–100, at p. 97.

253 Mario I. Aguilar, *A Social History of the Catholic Church in Chile, Vol. III: The Second Period of the Pinochet Government 1980–1990*, Lewiston, Queenston and Lampeter: Edwin Mellen Press, 2006, p. 115.

254 Nancy Cardoso Pereira, 'The Immobile Dance: The Body and the Bible in Latin America', in Regina Ammicht-Quinn and Elsa Tamez (eds), *The Body and Religion* (*Concilium* 2002/2), London: SCM Press, pp. 76–83, at pp. 82–3.

255 John McGuire Downey, 'Amazonia and the Fellowship Campaign', *Comboni Mission* Spring 2007, pp. 6–7. For other related activism in Brazil, including the Landless Workers Movement (*MST*), see Tomás Balduino, 'The Struggle for a Just Land Policy', in José Oscar Beozzo and Luiz Carlos Susin (eds), *Brazil: People and Church[es]* (*Concilium* 2002/3), London: SCM Press, pp. 54–60. The *MST, Movimento dos Trabalhadores Rurais Sem Terra*, is the largest social movement in Latin America with an estimated 1.5 million members present in 23 out of 27 states of Brazil. Officially established in 1984, the *MST* advocates social actions for land reform following the 1988 Brazilian Constitution that, in article 184, provides for agrarian reform and specifically for land expropriation as a social function of the Brazilian State.

256 Pedro Casaldáliga and José María Vigil, *The Spirituality of Liberation*, Liberation and Theology 12, Tunbridge Wells: Burns & Oates, 1994, p. 100.

257 José M. Castillo, 'Utopia Set Aside', in Luiz Carlos Susin, Jon Sobrino and Felix Wilfred (eds), *A Different World Is Possible* (*Concilium* 2004/5), London: SCM Press, pp. 35–41.

258 Gustavo Gutiérrez, *On Job: God-Talk and the Suffering of the Innocent*, Maryknoll, NY: Orbis, 1987, p. 103.

259 Manuel Antonio Garretón, Marcelo Cavarozzi, Peter S. Cleaves, Gary Gereffi and Jonathan Hartlyn, *América Latina en el siglo XXI:*

Hacia una nueva matriz sociopolítica, Santiago: LOM, 2004, pp. 81–2.

260 Dom Helder Cámara, *Church and Colonialism*, London and Sidney: Sheed & Ward, 1969.

261 José María Vigil, 'The God of War and the God of Peace with Justice', in María Pilar Aquino and Dietmar Mieth (eds), *The Return of the Just War* (*Concilium* 2001/2), London: SCM Press, pp. 94–101, at p. 99.

262 Lisa Sowle Cahill, 'Christian Just War Tradition: Tensions and Development', in Aquino and Mieth (eds), *Return of the Just War*, pp. 74–82, at p. 82.

263 Before 9/11 financial comparisons and the state of social injustice in the world were measured according to consumption rather than international security; however, the message was the same: there is a sinful distribution of resources, a dis-grace in the words of Frei Betto, who at that time pointed out that 'According to the UNICEF report on the state of the world's children in 2000, some 500,000,000 children live below the poverty line. To obtain, within a decade, access for these children to education, reducing poverty and eliminating child labour, would need an investment of US$7 billion – the equivalent of what Europeans spend on ice cream in one year' (in Frei Betto, 'Grace in the Midst of Dis-grace: Unexpected Gifts', in Ellen van Wolde (ed.), *The Bright Side of Life* (*Concilium* 2000/4), London: SCM Press, pp. 98–105, at p. 101).

264 Thomas Merton to Ernesto Cardenal, 10 March 1964, in Christine M. Bochen (ed.), *The Courage for Truth: The Letters of Thomas Merton to Writers*, New York: Farrar, Straus & Giroux, 1993, p. 144.

Chapter 9

265 Most of the ongoing themes and debates within Latin American theology are summarized in the entries within the compendium by Ignacio Ellacuría and Jon Sobrino (eds), *Mysterium liberationis: Fundamental Concepts of Liberation Theology*, Maryknoll, NY: Orbis, 1993; Iván Petrella, *The Future of Liberation Theology: An Argument and Manifesto*, Aldershot and Burlington, VT: Ashgate, 2004; and Marcella Althaus-Reid, *From Feminist Theology to Indecent Theology*, London: SCM Press, 2004.

266 Juan Luis Segundo, 'Two Theologies of Liberation', Toronto, 22 March 1983, in Alfred T. Hennelly (ed.), *Liberation Theology: A Documentary History*, Maryknoll, NY: Orbis, 1990, pp. 353–66.

267 I refer here to the reality of the successful marketing of books on liberation theology within the English-speaking world so that in the interpretation by Althaus-Reid 'unfortunately, a tourist theological

industry existed and created much confusion, in the sense that this industry became part of an academy imaginary': see Marcella Althaus-Reid, *From Feminist Theology to Indecent Theology*, London: SCM Press, 2004, p. 131.

268 See Clodovis Boff, 'Epistemology and Method of the Theology of Liberation', in Ellacuría and Sobrino (eds), *Mysterium liberationis*, pp. 57–85, and Ronaldo Muñoz, 'Option for the Poor', in Virginia Fabella and R. S. Sugirtharajah (eds), *Dictionary of Third World Theologies*, Maryknoll, NY: Orbis, 2000, pp. 154–6.

269 Some of the theoretical themes have been reassessed within Iván Petrella (ed.), *Latin American Theology: The Next Generation*, Maryknoll, NY: Orbis, 2005.

270 Gustavo Gutiérrez, *On Job: God-Talk and the Suffering of the Innocent*, Maryknoll, NY: Orbis, 1987, p. 102.

271 Gutiérrez, *On Job*, p. xix.

272 For Elsa Tamez, see Mario I. Aguilar, *The History and Politics of Latin American Theology*, Volume I, London: SCM Press, 2007; Volume II, London: SCM Press, 2008; for Frei Betto, see some of his narratives about his time in prison, in Frei Betto, 'Grace in the Midst of Dis-grace: Unexpected Gifts', in Ellen van Wolde (ed.), *The Bright Side of Life* (*Concilium* 2000/4), London: SCM Press, pp. 98–105.

273 Althaus-Reid, *From Feminist Theology to Indecent Theology*, p. 74.

274 For a rare example of this kind of theological genre, see Ernesto Cardenal, *La revolución perdida: Memorias III*, Mexico: Fondo de Cultura Económica, 2005.

275 I have outlined the historical developments of this period in Chilean history in Mario I. Aguilar, *A Social History of the Catholic Church in Chile, Vol. I: The First Period of the Pinochet Government 1973–1980*, Lewiston, Queenston and Lampeter: Edwin Mellen Press, 2004.

276 For a theological analysis of the diversity of monotheism in Christianity and Islam, see Claude Geffré, 'The One God of Islam and Trinitarian Monotheism', in Werner Jeanrond and Christoph Theobald (eds), *God: Experience and Mystery* (*Concilium* 2001/1), London: SCM Press, pp. 85–93.

277 Mario I. Aguilar, 'Dialogue with Waso Boorana Traditional Religious Practices', *African Ecclesial Review* 35/2, 1993, pp. 101–14; 'Current Waso Boorana Religious Practices: The *Kairos* for Inter-Religious Dialogue', *Verbum SVD* 34 /2, 1993, pp. 157–70; 'The Social Experience of Two Gods in Africa', *African Ecclesial Review* 36/1, 1994, pp. 32–44; and 'Dialogue with Islam: An African Perspective', *African Ecclesial Review* 38/6, 1996, pp. 322–40.

278 I have described all these practices in Mario I. Aguilar, *Being Oromo in Kenya*, Trenton, NJ: Africa World Press, 1998.

279 Mario I. Aguilar, 'El Muro de los Nombres de Villa Grimaldi (Chile): Exploraciones sobre la Memoria, el Silencio y la Voz de la Historia', *European Review of Latin American and Caribbean Studies* 69, 2000, pp. 81–8, and 'The Ethnography of the Villa Grimaldi in Pinochet's Chile: From Public Landscape to Secret Detention Centre (1973–1980)', *Iberoamericana* 18, 2005, pp. 7–23.

280 William T. Cavanaugh, *Torture and Eucharist: Theology, Politics and the Body of Christ*, Oxford: Blackwell, 1998.

281 José M. Castillo, 'Utopia Set Aside', in Luiz Carlos Susin, Jon Sobrino and Felix Wilfred (eds), *A Different World Is Possible* (*Concilium* 2004/5), London: SCM Press, pp. 35–41.

282 Jon Sobrino, 'Redeeming Globalization through Its Victims', in Jon Sobrino and Felix Wilfred (eds), *Globalization and Its Victims* (*Concilium* 2001/5), London: SCM Press, pp. 105–14, at p. 107.

283 Cardenal, *La revolución perdida: Memorias III*, p. 340.

284 Leonardo Boff, *The Lord Is My Shepherd: Divine Consolation in Times of Abandonment*, Maryknoll, NY: Orbis, 2006, p. 24.

285 Mario I. Aguilar, 'Los rosales de la humanidad', unpublished poem, March 2007.

286 A month before his arrest Alvaro Barrios had married Gabriela Zúñiga Figueroa and I am grateful to her for sharing some of her memories when we met in Santiago on 20 September 2006.

287 One of his famous poems, 'O Captain! My Captain!', was used in the film *Dead Poets Society* (1989), a classic film about poetry, with Robin Williams as its main character, a teacher who loved poetry in an East Coast boys' prep school.

288 Adam Feinstein, *Pablo Neruda: A Passion for Life*, London: Bloomsbury, 2005, pp. 213, 292, 308, 336, 386.

289 John Dear, 'The God of Peace Is Never Glorified by Human Violence: Keynote Address to the International Thomas Merton Society, June, 2005', in Victor A. Kramer and David Belcastro (eds), *The Merton Annual: Studies in Culture, Spirituality and Social Concerns* 19, Louisville, KY: Fons Vitae, 2006, pp. 24–38, at p. 29.

290 I support Iván Petrella's efforts to address the ills of capitalism through a liberation theology that pays attention to 'the literature on comparative political economy'. Unlike him, however, I remain sceptical about the possibility of theologizing in theoretical traits that do not integrate faith communities or the liberating action of God within the contra-capitalism discourse. See Iván Petrella, 'Liberation Theology – a Programmatic Statement', in Iván Petrella (ed.), *Latin American Theology*, pp. 147–72, at p. 162. I tend to agree with Eugenio Tironi,

who has argued that Chile as a democratic state is fully inserted not in the old European world but in the US 'universe': see Eugenio Tironi, *Crónica de viaje: Chile y la ruta a la felicidad*, Santiago: Empresa El Mercurio and Aguilar Chilena de Ediciones, 2006, p. 251.

Index

Index

Colegio del Verbo Divino
(Santiago) 188n. 7
Comblin, José 101
acceptance of interfaith
dialogue 105
on the introduction of politics
into Christian ritual 75
on migration from urban
centres 143
on Pentecostalist theology
110–11
on political disinterest 156–7
common good, individuals
subordinated to 40
communism, John Paul II's
attitudes to 1, 187n. 3
community, concept of 72
Congregation for the Doctrine
of the Faith (CDF), Ratzinger
appointed prefect of 2
consumerism 117–18, 121
denial of the values of the
Kingdom of God 122–3
dominance 29–30
monasticism's challenges to
124–6
and political disinterest 157
sinfulness of 128–9, 130–1
contextual backgrounds, in
Latin American theology
171–5, 177–8, 185–6
contrarieties, in theology 6,
13–15
'contrarieties of Israel' 6
COPACHI 104
Cordingley, Patrick, Major
General 168
Cuscatlán battalion (El
Salvador), participation in
the Iraq war 141

Dalai Lama, views on
humanity 118, 203n. 185
De Carrillo, Beatrice, on El
Salvador's participation in
the Iraq war 141
de la Serna, Eduardo, on
Christianity in crisis 102
de Las Casas, Bartolomé 18
Dead Poets Society (film)
212n. 287
Dear, John, on non-violence
184–5
democracy, influence on
models of the Kingdom of
God 92
denarii 195n. 87
dialogic imagination 49–50
disciples and discipleship
in Mark 48, 50, 51–2
post-resurrection ministry
62–3
see also Galilean 12
Dominus Iesus 107
Donatists 55, 125
Drummel, Werner (European
Union Ambassador in Mexico
and Austrian Ambassador),
opposition to construction of
border wall between the US
and Mexico 144
Dulles, Avery, on Church
models 86, 93, 95
Dussel, Enrique 187n. 5
on centre-periphery conflicts
in theology 67
theological and social practice
18
use of centre-periphery
models 66
work within the periphery 36

Index

Index

and the centre 31–5
  in Mark 58–63
effects of globalization 137
effects of the internet 136–7
fellowship in 95
Galilee as 43–4
  in Jesus' ministry 47, 48–9,
  51
and globalization 135
human commonality in
  118–19
importance for development
  of Latin American theology
  185–6
inclusion in political activism
  158, 159–60
inhabitants excluded from
  economic prosperity 42
interfaith dialogue 101,
  104–6, 108–9, 115
location in theology 26–9
mapping of 33–6
political activism in 165
poverty in 39–40, 119–20
realization of the Kingdom of
  God 40–1
spirituality of liberation in
  127–9
theologians' work within
  36–8
theological role 3, 4–5,
  15–16, 17, 19–20, 25–6
theologizing in 95–9, 102–3
theology 6–7, 9–10, 14–20
  realization 41
see also centre; centre-
  periphery
Peter (disciple)
  challenged as a Galilean 48
  in Mark's Gospel 57–8

Petrella, Iván 3, 142
  author's disagreements with
  33
  on capitalism and liberation
  theology 212n. 290
  on the Church in civil society
  93–4
  liberation theology 10–11
  theological contextual
  background 173
pilgrimages *see caminata*
Pinochet Ugarte, Augusto,
  attempted assassination of
  96–7
poetry, use in theologizing
  180–3
political activism
  and Christian utopia 157–64,
  165, 177
  peaceful objectives 164–9
  post-military dictatorships
  153–7
  silencing of 164–5
  theology 152–3
political disinterest 156–7
political theology, and
  theology of the political 3,
  189n. 10
politicization, in Jesus' ministry
  52–3, 54–5
politics, introduction into
  Christian ritual 75
the poor
  biblical hermeneutics 46
  Church's involvement with
  91–2, 200n. 139
  conscription 185
  God's concerns for to be
  reflected in the Church
  86–8